A Teacher's Guide to Working With

# Children
# &Families

## From Diverse Backgrounds

*A CEC-TAG Educational Resource*

A Teacher's Guide to Working With

# Children & Families

## From Diverse Backgrounds

### *A CEC-TAG Educational Resource*

*Julia Link Roberts, Ed.D., & Jennifer L. Jolly, Ph.D.*

Series Editors
Cheryll M. Adams, Ph.D., Tracy L. Cross, Ph.D.,
Susan K. Johnsen, Ph.D., and Diane Montgomery, Ph.D.

PRUFROCK PRESS INC.
WACO, TEXAS

Library of Congress Cataloging-in-Publication Data

Roberts, Julia L. (Julia Link) author.
 A teacher's guide to working with children and families from diverse backgrounds : a CEC-TAG educational resource / By Julia Link Roberts, Ed.D., & Jennifer L. Jolly, Ph.D.
    pages cm
Includes bibliographical references.
ISBN 978-1-59363-916-7 (pbk.)
1. Gifted children--Education. 2. Children with social disabilities--Education. I. Jolly, Jennifer L., 1972- author. II. Title.
LC3993.R6124 2012
371.95--dc23
                        2012014874

Edited by Jennifer Robins

Layout Design by Marjorie Parker and Raquel Trevino

ISBN-13: 978-1-59363-916-7

Printed in the United States of America.

Prufrock Press Inc.
P.O. Box 8813
Waco, TX 76714-8813
Phone: (800) 998-2208
Fax: (800) 240-0333
http://www.prufrock.com

# Table of Contents

# CHAPTER 1

# Barriers to Recognizing Talent Among Diverse Children With Gifts and Talents

All of us do not have equal talent, but all of us should have an equal opportunity to develop our talents.

—John F. Kennedy

When parents and educators collaborate, they increase the likelihood that children will thrive in school. They can work together to set high goals for *all* children, including those from diverse backgrounds who are also gifted and talented or who have the potential to be advanced learners. Every child in every classroom must have ongoing opportunities to learn on a daily basis. An important component of ongoing learning is to have an appropriate level of challenge. In the context of learning, appropriate challenge is very much like the story of *Goldilocks and the Three Bears*: The teacher must plan what is "just right" in terms of challenging children—not too easy and not too hard. Educators must ensure that they provide opportunities for all children to learn new things every day. School must be the place where children acquire the habits of lifelong learners: they ask questions, they pursue learning opportunities with interest, and they think at high levels. Students thrive when they are involved in engaging learning experiences that encourage them to make continuous progress.

Diversity is an important topic that can expand many discussions about children with gifts and talents. The Association for the Gifted, a division of the Council for Exceptional Children (CEC-TAG), included "race, culture, ethnicity, class, gender, sexual orientation, and linguistic issues" within the topic of diversity (CEC-TAG, 2009, p. 3). Diverse learners include children who are culturally, linguistically, and ethnically diverse as well as children who have multiple exceptionalities (e.g., a student can be gifted and also have a learning disability). Frequently, educators overlook diverse children for gifted and talented identification and services, resulting in their strengths going unnoticed or being underdeveloped or misunderstood. "This underrepresentation belies the premise that the capacity for exceptional achievement exists across racial, ethnic, language, and economic groups as well as some categories of disability" (CEC-TAG, 2009, p. 3).

# MYTHS THAT PRESENT BARRIERS

Myths about gifted children often interfere with educators' ability to recognize the exceptional abilities of diverse children who are gifted and talented, and those myths and misunderstandings further hinder the recognition of exceptional ability among children from lower income families, children from families who do not speak English as their first language, children from various cultural and/or ethnic backgrounds, children from rural and urban schools, and children who are twice-exceptional (i.e., have gifts and talents and also a disability or disabilities). Myths and misunderstandings frequently mask the potential of these children. There are numerous barriers for children who are diverse in one or more of the dimensions mentioned above and also have the potential to be advanced learners.

## BARRIER 1

Some educators may mistakenly think that gifted children are from middle- and upper income families. However, gifted children's families represent the full socioeconomic spectrum. The amount of financial resources a family has does not determine the potential for a child to learn at advanced levels, yet few individuals will recognize a gifted child who may qualify for free or reduced lunch unless they believe that children from all socioeconomic backgrounds can be gifted.

## BARRIER 2

Many educators may believe that children with disabilities cannot also be gifted. Children who are twice-exceptional can appear to be anything but gifted unless teachers carefully assess their strengths and teach to them. If teachers are unaware of the possibility that a child may be twice-exceptional, they will concentrate on addressing the needs created by the disability and overlook the needs created by the strengths, seriously limiting opportunities to develop the student's potential.

## BARRIER 3

Culturally diverse students may not display their gifts and talents in ways that mirror what teachers have traditionally been taught to use in recognizing advanced ability or potential. With these limitations, many gifted and talented children from culturally diverse families may not even be considered for advanced instruction or nomination for placement in gifted programming due to a mismatch between perceived expectations and actual or potential performance. Many educators also expect English language learners (ELLs; children for whom English is not the first language in their home) to be preoccupied with learning to speak and read English. Instead, ELLs may be frustrated by limitations presented in the curriculum, as they need to think at high levels but don't have opportunities to do so. Their needs are twofold: the need to acquire fluency in English and the need to be learning at a challenging level in the different content areas.

## BARRIER 4

The focus on grade-level learning or proficiency raises a barrier to learning for children who are ready to learn at a faster pace and at a more complex level. All children who are ready to progress as readers

## TABLE 1
## TRUTHS ABOUT GIFTED CHILDREN

- Families of children with gifts and talents represent high-, middle-, and low-income levels.
- Children with gifts and talents may also have disabilities, and these children are twice-exceptional.
- Children with gifts and talents include all cultural and ethnic backgrounds.
- In order to make continuous progress, children with gifts and talents need ongoing learning experiences with no learning ceiling.
- Gifted children become underachievers, drop out of school, and fail to reach their potential when they are not challenged.

or to absorb more advanced content in science or history, for example, need opportunities to do so rather than having to wait until others in the class share those interests or are ready to move on with the content. That may never happen, or it may not occur at a pace at which the advanced learners are eager to learn. Waiting until others are "ready" can create bad habits that lead to situational or long-term underachievement.

### BARRIER 5

Probably the greatest barrier is that so many people, including educators, believe that there is no need to worry about children with gifts and talents, as they will "make it" on their own. Contrary to that prevalent myth (and it *is* a myth), children do not thrive in school when it is believed that they will be fine even in classrooms that provide little or no challenge. Many will become underachievers, and this is a pattern that is very difficult to reverse.

Despite the prevalence of the mythology about children with gifts and talents, truths about these exceptional children will be shared in the chapters of this book. Table 1 enumerates truths that inform educators who may previously have thought the myths were factual.

# COLLABORATION

This book is written for educators, although it may be useful for parents, too. Genuine collaboration begins when educators and parents share information about a child—his interests, strengths, and passions. What does she do with her time when not in school? What books does he read when he has a choice? What television programs does she watch that indicate her interest in a particular topic? What does he talk about when he has the opportunity to open a conversation about a topic or topics that are important to him? Such sharing provides a sound foundation for understanding a child.

Parents and other family members want what is best for their children. They want them to have a good life, and they want them to be prepared for success in life (however they define that). Educators also want the young people they teach to be successful, underscoring why working together is so important for both educators and parents. To collaborate effectively, educators need to work with families and plan for the child's ongoing learning and educational opportunities. It is important to remember that good communication includes listening as well as talking.

Whose responsibility is it to initiate a meeting between the parents and the educator? There is no right answer to this question, but either party should step forward if it thinks there is a need to learn more about what is—or is not—occurring at school, whichever the case may be. Parents may recognize behaviors and conversations that signal a need to talk with the teacher or other educators at the school. On the other hand, teachers may have concerns that need to be shared, or they may have noticed strengths they want to communicate to the parents. Collaboration is a two-way street, and the focal points may be an issue to resolve or a strategy to build on the child's strengths. Together parents and teachers can work together for the benefit of the child.

Two goals for collaboration are success for children and talent development for them. What do these goals mean for children with gifts and talents?

## GOAL 1: ACADEMIC SUCCESS

Of course, planning for success is important for all children. What might be considered success? It is important to think about that question, as the answer will guide decisions and choices for what teachers plan for students to learn. If it is success in school, then is success defined in terms of all "A" grades, or is it also a matter of learning at challenging levels? Is success understood to be reaching challenging learning goals with hard work and effort? Is success understood to be lifelong learning? Are young people successful if they develop into analytical and creative thinkers and problem solvers?

Figure 1 describes the different levels of academic success (Roberts, 2008). Perhaps an important conversation between teachers and parents would concern their understanding of academic success. Both teachers and parents need to consider the various levels of academic success. Getting stuck on the lowest rung of the ladder of academic success can be short-sighted. Good grades and high praise for work that is easy for children (Level 1) will not prepare them for challenge as they progress through school. Level 2, in which good grades are combined with effort, will step up the level of preparation that children have for tackling challenging academic tasks. All students need to break an academic sweat—just as athletes must do—if they are to improve their skills and perform at increasingly higher levels. Level 3 is where students need to be by the time they leave school, and at that level they will continue to learn for a lifetime.

Success also may be defined as readiness to perform at high levels in postsecondary opportunities, whether that means in college or other postsecondary learning environments. Being successful beyond high school is likely to be closely related to appropriate preparation, which includes taking advanced courses throughout the school experience, especially during high school. Courses should require students to think at high levels (both critically and creatively) and to develop an academic work ethic in order to do well. Study skills must be developed, and students must have a need to study in order to hone these skills. Likewise, young people do not become 21st-century learners by achieving mastery within a fact-based, recall curriculum. Learners prepared to do well in the 21st century will be critical and creative thinkers who are effective at both teamwork and working independently. They will be adaptable and able to acquire new skills needed for new situations and for new positions in which they may find themselves. Athletes do not succeed in a marathon without preparation. That is also true for young people preparing to be successful in postsecondary opportunities and careers.

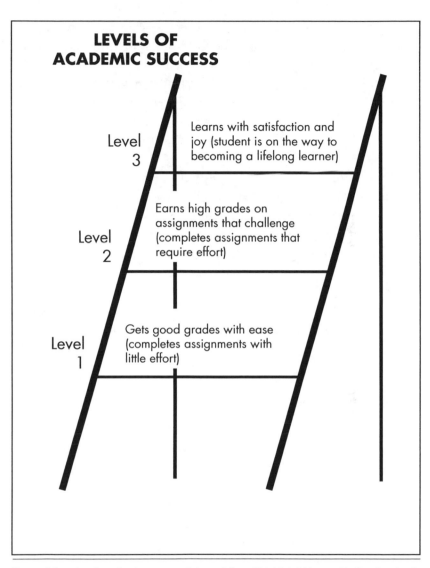

*Figure 1.* Levels of academic success. Adapted from "Multiple Ways to Define Academic Success: What Resonates With You?" by J. L. Roberts, 2008, *The Challenge, 21,* p. 13. Adapted with permission.

## GOAL 2: TALENT DEVELOPMENT

An underlying assumption in this book is that both teachers and parents have great opportunities to be talent developers. Talent development, hopefully, begins at home and continues in elementary, middle, and high school classrooms. In an ideal situation, both educators and parents recognize budding interests and talents and work together to promote their development. Talents do not burst into a child's life but rather develop over time. They are encouraged by teachers and coaches and prepare a child to be ready for opportunities as they present themselves or are offered.

On a recent trip to Florence, Italy (taken by the first author), an art historian pointed out a few early works of Michelangelo, all of which those viewing the pieces considered to be exceptional. Then the art historian highlighted pieces that Michelangelo produced much later in his career to illustrate how much his talent had developed after years of working on his techniques and expression. The message was that no person first demonstrates his talents and abilities at the highest level at which he is capable of performing. Development continues with plenty of hard work and opportunities that are focused on the development of talent.

# OVERVIEW OF THE BOOK

Schools are increasingly diverse in their student populations, presenting new challenges for teachers. In light of these challenges, schools remain important in preparing young people for success in postsecondary opportunities and in the talent development process. *A Teacher's Guide to Working With Children and Families From Diverse Backgrounds* provides important information and strategies for educators at all levels. The book is written for educators who want all children to thrive in school, including those who are twice-exceptional, those from lower income backgrounds, and others who have been underrepresented in gifted programming. The target audience is educators who want to develop the talents of children and young people in their classrooms and schools.

Tools for educators will be included throughout the book to provide resources to enhance understanding of diverse learners with high potential. Each chapter will include a "Tools for Digging Deeper" section that features books, websites, and other resources that will help educators learn—and perhaps share with parents!

# TOOLS FOR DIGGING DEEPER

Common Gifted Education Myths
http://www.nagc.org/commonmyths.aspx
The National Association for Gifted Children (NAGC) shares common myths—and truths—about gifted children.

*Gifted Child Quarterly*
http://gcq.sagepub.com
The Fall 2009 issue of *Gifted Child Quarterly* focuses on myths. More than 30 years ago (Winter 1982), another issue of the journal was dedicated to myths, highlighting the fact that myths persist over time. Both issues are valuable resources for learning about what is fact or fiction regarding children who are gifted and talented.

Top 10 Myths in Gifted Education
http://www.msde.maryland.gov/MSDE/programs/giftedtalented/top_ten_myths_video
This 8-minute video was produced by teens in Baltimore County Public Schools for the Maryland State Department of Education.

Inman, T. F. (Winter, 2007). What a child doesn't learn. *The Challenge, 18,* 17–19.
This article discusses what a child for whom school is easy misses out on learning that other children learn because they are required to work hard in elementary school.

# CHAPTER 2

# Gifted Education and Talent Development: An Overview

We are altogether too easily deceived by the time-worn argument that the gifted student, "the genius" perhaps, will get along somehow without much teaching. The fact is, the gifted . . . and the brilliant . . . are the ones who need the closest attention of the skilful [*sic*] mechanic.

—W. Franklin Jones

In order to collaborate effectively, it is important for educators to have some basic information about gifted education and talent development, information they can share with parents. This information provides the backdrop for successful collaboration. This chapter includes definitions of giftedness and talent development, characteristics of children with gifts and talents, federal guidelines for special needs learners, and the rights of gifted children. Information about these topics could fill a book, but only a few basics are presented—basics needed for parents and educators to collaborate about children who are sometimes, if not often, overlooked for gifted programming. Those who are overlooked most often are children who come from diverse backgrounds—those who represent lower income families, those who are culturally diverse, and those who are twice-exceptional. Still other children with gifts and talents are in classrooms in which teachers impose a learning ceiling when they assume that gifted children will "make it on their own." Teachers need basic information about children with gifts and talents in order to avoid believing myths that are held by many people.

# DEFINITIONS OF GIFTEDNESS

As teachers prepare to talk with parents about giftedness and/or talent development, it would be useful to have some common understandings. Definitions provide an important place to begin such discussions. There is no one definition of gifted children that is used across the United States, as states establish their own definitions. Although there are a couple of national definitions, each state has its own definition that may or may not mirror one of the national definitions.

The definition presented in the Jacob K. Javits Gifted and Talented Students Education Act (1988) is:

> Children and youth with outstanding talent perform or show the potential for performing at remarkably high levels of accomplishment when compared with others of their age, experience, or environment. These children and youth exhibit high performance capability in intellectual, creative, and/or artistic areas, possess an unusual leadership capacity, or excel in specific academic fields. They require services or activities not ordinarily provided by the schools. Outstanding talents are present in children and youth from all cultural groups, across all economic strata, and in all areas of human endeavor. (U.S. Department of Education, 1993, p. 3)

Several points in this definition are key to understanding diversity among gifted learners. The phrase "performing at remarkably high levels of accomplishment when compared with others of their age, experience, or environment" is important to those working with diverse children of exceptional potential. Any comparison of children does not need to be made with *all* children of a particular age but with children of *comparable* experiences and in similar environments. Likewise, the definition states, "Outstanding talents are present in children and youth from all cultural groups, across all economic strata." The key to increasing the understanding of giftedness among diverse learners and eliminating mythology is to educate families and educators so they will recognize giftedness, including giftedness among diverse learners with gifts and talents.

In the Elementary and Secondary Education Act, known as No Child Left Behind, the following definition of gifted and talented is provided:

> The term "gifted and talented," when used with respect to students, children, or youth, means students, children, or youth who give evidence of high achievement capability in areas such as intellectual, creative, artistic, or leadership capacity, or in specific academic fields, and who need services or activities not ordinarily provided by the school in order to fully develop those capabilities. (No Child Left Behind Act, P.L. 107-110 [Title IX, Part A, Definition 22], 2002)

Both federal definitions provide a wide lens for viewing and recognizing gifts and talents among children and young people. The definitions specify that children may be gifted and talented in general intellectual ability or in a specific academic area such as mathematics, social studies, science, and/or language arts. They may also be gifted in creativity, leadership, and/or the visual or performing arts. It is important to note that students may be gifted in one or more of these categories. The inclusion of various categories of giftedness in the definitions is key to understanding the needs of children with gifts and talents. Needs for gifted and talented children stem from strengths rather than deficiencies. Consequently, gifted children do not look needy. Children with gifts and talents are just as different from an average child as a child who has special needs that stem from areas that require support. The needs of children with gifts and talents must be accommodated if they are to make continuous progress in school.

The National Association for Gifted Children (2010b) offered another definition in its position paper on redefining giftedness:

> Gifted individuals are those who demonstrate outstanding levels of aptitude (defined as an exceptional ability to reason and learn) or competence (documented performance or achievement in top 10% or rarer) in one or more domains. Domains include any structured area of activity with its own symbol system (e.g., mathematics, music, language) and/or set of sensorimotor skills (e.g., painting, dance, sports). (para. 4)

There is no national mandate for identifying and providing services for children with gifts and talents, so states are responsible for legislation and policy related to this population of children. Understanding the definition that is used in a particular school and/or district is essential in order to have a basic understanding of the terminology. Some states have chosen to use the term *advanced learners* or *high-ability learners* instead of children with gifts and talents or gifted and talented children. No matter what terminology is used, it only establishes the starting point for collaboration between educators and parents.

# SPECIFICITY IN REFERENCING STUDENTS WITH GIFTS AND TALENTS

A useful tip for referencing children who are gifted and talented is to be specific about the area(s) of gifts and talents. Frequently newspapers write about gifted athletes or gifted musicians. Although it seems quite acceptable to most people to use the term *gifted* with athletes, musicians, artists, and dancers, many people hesitate to use the term in regard to intellectual giftedness. The more specific the label, the more likely the term gifted is appreciated and readily used. For example, it is widely accepted to use the term gifted with a specific area of accomplishment (e.g., a gifted mathematician, gifted reader, gifted writer, gifted scientist). Doing so is also more easily understood by the child who is gifted in a specific academic or artistic area.

# DEFINITION OF TALENT DEVELOPMENT

The National Association for Gifted Children (2010b) published a position paper called *Redefining Giftedness for a New Century: Shifting the Paradigm* (see http://www.nagc.org/index.aspx?id=6404&terms=Redefin ing+giftedness). The focus of this statement is on talent development.

The development of ability or talent is a lifelong process. It can be evident in young children as exceptional performance on tests and/or other measures of ability, or as a rapid rate of learning, compared to other students of the same age, or in actual achievement in a domain. As individuals mature through childhood to adolescence, however, achievement and high levels of motivation in the domain become the primary characteristics of their giftedness. Various factors can either enhance or inhibit the development and expression of abilities. (para. 5)

The last sentence in this statement is the most important to the topic of this book: whether or not children develop their talents depends on opportunities to do so. Strategies must be in place to develop talent among children with gifts and talents, including diverse children who are often underrepresented in programming, or such talent may not ever develop. Talent development will be inhibited without opportunities to make continuous progress in a talent area. On the other hand, appropriate opportunities can lead to developing talent at increasingly higher levels. Talent development is not automatic; rather, it occurs when educators and parents provide learning opportunities that foster talent development.

# CHARACTERISTICS OF CHILDREN WITH GIFTS AND TALENTS

Many states recognize giftedness in several domains, and others limit their definition to intellectually or academically gifted children. The most all-encompassing definition of giftedness recognizes various categories of accomplishment or high potential. One may be gifted intellectually or in a specific academic area (e.g., language arts, mathematics, social studies, science). One may also be recognized as gifted in creativity, leadership, and/or the visual or performing arts.

No one set of characteristics describes all children with gifts and talents in general or in any one of those categories. However, there are characteristics that are typical of children and that demonstrate outstanding ability or the potential for exceptional performance in the various categories. It is highly unlikely that a child will have all of the characteristics, yet sometimes such a listing of characteristics proves to be useful in recognizing exceptional talent. Figure 2 provides a listing of characteristics that are frequently found to describe children who are gifted and talented in the various categories of giftedness and high potential.

# FEDERAL LEGISLATION RECOGNIZES CHILDREN WITH GIFTS AND TALENTS

The Higher Education Opportunity Act (2008) specifies the priority of preparing teachers with teaching skills that

> focus on the identification of students' specific learning needs, particularly students with disabilities, students who are limited English proficient, students who are gifted and talented, and students with low literacy levels, and the tailoring of academic instruction to such needs. (pp. 3132–3133)

This legislation highlights specific learning needs and includes the needs of gifted children in that listing. Of course, it is possible for children to be gifted and also have a disability, gifted and have limited English proficiency, and gifted and exhibit low literacy levels. Each type of learner singled out in the Higher Education Opportunity Act has specific learning needs. These needs must be addressed in elementary, middle, and high school classrooms if these children are to survive and thrive. Educators must understand that gifted children have learning needs that are created by their strengths; consequently, they may not look needy. Nonetheless, their needs are real and must be addressed if they are going to develop their potential. Educators must understand, too, that it is possible to have learning needs in various combinations. These understandings comprise a few of the basics for successful collaboration between parents and educators concerning children with gifts and talents.

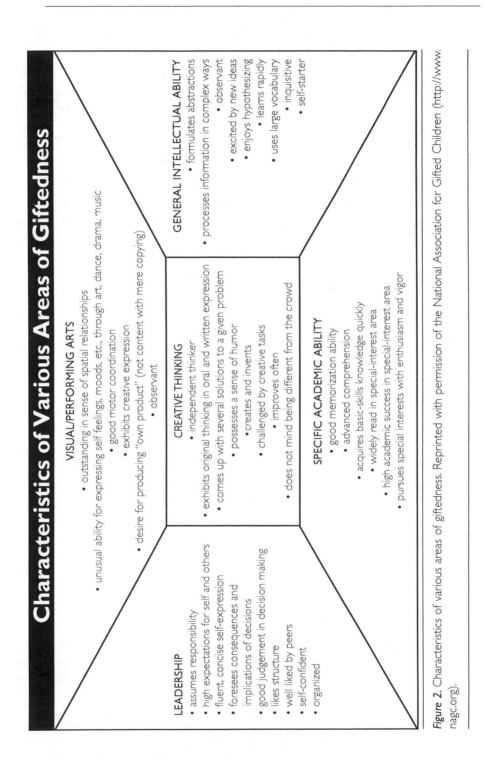

# Characteristics of Various Areas of Giftedness

## VISUAL/PERFORMING ARTS
- unusual ability for expressing self feelings, moods, etc., through art, dance, drama, music
- outstanding in sense of spatial relationships
- good motor coordination
- exhibits creative expression
- desire for producing "own product" (not content with mere copying)
- observant

## GENERAL INTELLECTUAL ABILITY
- formulates abstractions
- processes information in complex ways
- observant
- excited by new ideas
- enjoys hypothesizing
- learns rapidly
- uses large vocabulary
- inquisitive
- self-starter

## CREATIVE THINKING
- independent thinker
- exhibits original thinking in oral and written expression
- comes up with several solutions to a given problem
- possesses a sense of humor
- creates and invents
- challenged by creative tasks
- improves often
- does not mind being different from the crowd

## SPECIFIC ACADEMIC ABILITY
- good memorization ability
- advanced comprehension
- acquires basic-skills knowledge quickly
- widely read in special-interest area
- high academic success in special-interest area
- pursues special interests with enthusiasm and vigor

## LEADERSHIP
- assumes responsibility
- high expectations for self and others
- fluent, concise self-expression
- foresees consequences and implications of decisions
- good judgement in decision making
- likes structure
- well liked by peers
- self-confident
- organized

*Figure 2.* Characteristics of various areas of giftedness. Reprinted with permission of the National Association for Gifted Children (http://www. nagc.org).

# THE GIFTED CHILDREN'S BILL OF RIGHTS

Solid collaboration is based on common goals for children with gifts and talents. In 2007, then-NAGC President Del Siegle presented the Gifted Children's Bill of Rights (see Figure 3), and this listing of 10 rights establishes important understandings about children with gifts and talents. Several of the points in this list of rights are frequently misunderstood, so the Gifted Children's Bill of Rights helps create a common ground for educators to discuss them with parents. Some of the rights are important for social-emotional development; for example, the right "to know about your giftedness" and the right "to feel good about your accomplishments." Other rights have academic benefits, like the right "to learn something new every day." Still other rights have both academic and social-emotional benefits— for example, the right "to have multiple peer groups and a variety of friends."

Being with others who are idea-mates (they may be the same age but also may be older children) aids both social-emotional development and academic development. It is important to have others who stimulate the children academically and who allow them to know that they are not alone in thinking a particular way about a topic or in caring about discussing that issue. If the children are reading a couple of levels above their age-mates or can understand math concepts intended for students above their grade level, they need academic peers with whom to learn and to advance their skills development. They need friends who share some of their interests. The Gifted Children's Bill of Rights offers sound advice and is both a great resource for families to share with their children and also a conversation-starter to set the stage for discussions that educators have with parents.

# OFFERING A VARIETY OF SERVICES RATHER THAN "THE GIFTED PROGRAM"

For a long time, schools and school districts planned and offered one program to address the needs of gifted children. As the definition of

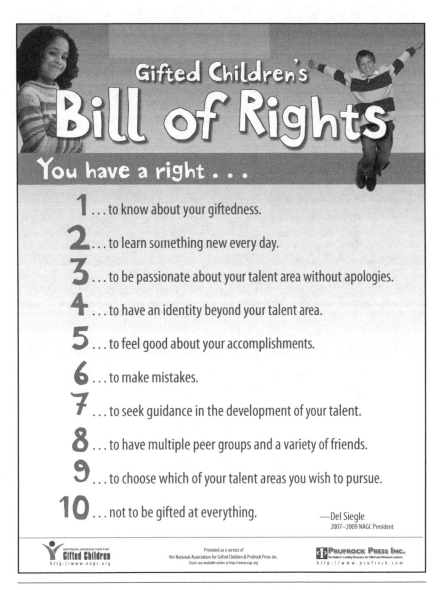

*Figure 3.* Gifted children's bill of rights. Reprinted with permission of the National Association for Gifted Children (http://www.nagc.org).

giftedness has broadened to include several categories—intellectual, academic, creative, leadership, and visual/performing arts—it is important
to plan programming and services to address the needs presented by each
category. Therefore, programming or services are terms used to communicate the need to match services with categories of giftedness. Educators
must consider and implement programs and services to accommodate
children who are gifted and talented and allow for continuous progress
in their strength areas. The term "the gifted program" is likely one service
and, hopefully, not the only service in a school. Consequently, it is useful
to call that pull-out or push-in service by a name such as Project SOAR
or the GEM Program to distinguish it from other services for children
with gifts and talents in the school. Programming or services for children
who are gifted and talented should be planned to develop the potential
of all children with gifts and talents, just as programming or services are
planned for other exceptional children. Various levels of programming
or services are needed to ensure that children who are exceptional have
opportunities to learn on an ongoing basis.

Services are most effective when they are planned to address specific
areas of giftedness or talent. For example, children who are advanced
in reading need a cluster group or a homogeneously grouped class of
students who are ready for a rapid pace for learning and more complex
content in reading. A cluster group would have 5–8 children who are
advanced readers in a class in which the teacher is experienced with differentiating instruction and is expected to differentiate instruction for the
cluster to advance their skills and interests in reading while others in the
classroom continue to make continuous progress in their reading as well.

Another way to provide services is through acceleration. "Acceleration
is an educational intervention that moves students through an education
program at a faster than usual rate or younger than typical age" (Colangelo,
Assouline, & Gross, 2004, p. 1). "Acceleration means matching the level,
complexity, and pace of instruction with the readiness and motivation
of the student" (Colangelo et al., 2004, p. 5). *A Nation Deceived: How
Schools Hold Back America's Brightest Children* (Colangelo et al., 2004)
enumerated 18 types of acceleration. Acceleration options can be divided
into two types: early entrance and curriculum-based. Table 2 provides a

## TABLE 2
## TYPES OF ACCELERATION

| Early Admissions | Curriculum-Based |
|---|---|
| 1. Early admission to kindergarten<br>2. Early admission to first grade<br>3. Grade-skipping<br>4. Early graduation<br>5. Concurrent/dual enrollment<br>6. Credit by examination<br>7. Acceleration into college<br>8. Early entrance into middle school, high school, or college | 1. Continuous progress<br>2. Self-paced instruction<br>3. Subject-matter acceleration/partial acceleration<br>4. Combined classes<br>5. Curriculum compacting<br>6. Telescoping curriculum<br>7. Mentoring<br>8. Extracurricular programs<br>9. Correspondence courses<br>10. Advanced Placement courses |

*Note.* Adapted from Southern and Jones (2004) with permission of authors.

listing of different ways that acceleration can be used to address learning needs and places them into the two categories.

Other service options include mentoring, independent study, a pull-out program, and differentiating the curriculum in the regular classroom. Services may take various forms, but the key to effective services is that they match student needs (which emanate from strengths in children with gifts and talents) and allow for continuous progress and/or talent development.

# THE NAGC PRE-K–GRADE 12 GIFTED PROGRAMMING STANDARDS

The NAGC Pre-K–Grade 12 Gifted Programming Standards (NAGC, 2010a) focus on student outcomes. The development of the standards was guided by five principles.

1. Giftedness is dynamic and is constantly developing; therefore, students are defined as those with gifts and talents rather than those with stable traits.

2.  Giftedness is found among students from a variety of back-
    grounds; therefore, a deliberate effort was made to ensure
    that diversity was included across all standards. Diversity
    was defined as differences among groups of people and indi-
    viduals based on ethnicity, race, socioeconomic status, gen-
    der, exceptionalities, language, religion, sexual orientation,
    and geographical area.
3.  Standards should focus on student outcomes rather than
    practices. The number of practices used or how they are used
    is not as important as whether or not the practice is effective
    with students. Consequently, the workgroup decided not to
    identify acceptable vs. exemplary standards. Moreover, such
    a distinction would be difficult to support with the research.
4.  Because all educators are responsible for the education
    of students with gifts and talents, educators were broadly
    defined as administrators, teachers, counselors, and other
    instructional support staff from a variety of professional
    backgrounds (e.g., general education, special education, and
    gifted education).
5.  Students with gifts and talents should receive services through-
    out the day and in all environments based on their abilities,
    needs, and interests. Therefore, the workgroup decided to use
    the word "programming" rather than the word "program,"
    which might connote a one-dimensional approach (e.g., a
    once-a-week type of program option). (p. 4)

The standards can be used in multiple ways. They can guide curriculum planning as well as the assessing, evaluating, and improving of
programming within a school or district. They also are useful in planning professional development, selecting educators, and advocating for
children with gifts and talents. The six standards focus on learning and
development, assessment, curriculum and instruction, learning environments, programming, and professional development.

Johnsen (2011b) stated that the new standards "reflect a much stronger emphasis on diversity . . . Because students from diverse backgrounds
continue to be underrepresented in gifted education programs, this

emphasis is critical for their inclusion and their ability to access quality programming" (p. 12).

# CONCLUDING THOUGHTS

This chapter provided some basic information about gifted education to initiate conversations with parents and guardians of diverse learners with gifts and talents. The information included definitions of gifted and talented children as well as of talent development. Characteristics of children were listed for those who are gifted intellectually and academically as well as in creativity, leadership, and the visual and performing arts. The Gifted Children's Bill of Rights helped to highlight important goals for children with gifts and talents. Services for gifted children were introduced in order to enhance understanding of options that educators can consider as they collaborate to address the needs of children with gifts and talents. Finally, the new NAGC Pre-K–Grade 12 Programming Standards provided the blueprint for planning, implementing, and assessing gifted programming within a school or district as well as for guiding the hiring of personnel and the providing of professional development.

# TOOLS FOR DIGGING DEEPER

*The NAGC Mile Marker Series*
http://www.nagc.org/NAGCMileMarker.aspx
This CD-ROM provides a variety of resources to help educators and parents learn about gifted children.

Jolly, J. L, Treffinger, D. J., Inman, T. F., & Smutny, J. F. (Eds.). (2010). *Parenting gifted children: The authoritative guide from the National Association for Gifted Children.* Waco, TX: Prufrock Press.
This book includes leading articles from issues of *Parenting for High Potential*, a magazine for parents published by the National Association for Gifted Children. The articles highlight a variety of topics of interest to parents as well as educators.

Roberts, J. L., & Boggess, J. R. (2011). *Teacher's survival guide: Gifted education.* Waco, TX: Prufrock Press.
This book introduces key information about gifted education to teachers.

# CHAPTER 3

# Gifted Students From Lower Income Families

Most teachers waste their time by asking questions which are intended to discover what a pupil does not know whereas the true art of questioning has for its purpose to discover what the pupil knows or is capable of knowing.

—Albert Einstein

Children who are gifted and talented come from families at all income levels. The challenge is that people who do not believe that to be true often fail to recognize the strengths and talents of children from lower income backgrounds. When that is the case, talented children enter school—perhaps in the upper quartile—and lose ground if their achievements are not recognized and developed (Wyner, Bridgeland, & DiIulio, 2007). According to Wyner et al.'s (2007) report entitled *Achievement Trap*, the potential of these children is jeopardized as many of them fail to thrive in school.

Today in America, there are millions of students who are overcoming challenging socioeconomic circumstances to excel academically. They defy the stereotype that poverty precludes high academic performance and that lower-income and low academic achievement are inextricably linked. They demonstrate that economically disadvantaged children can learn at the highest levels and provide hope to other lower-income students seeking to follow the same path.

Sadly, from the time they enter grade school through their postsecondary education, these students lose more educational ground and excel less frequently than their higher-income peers. Despite this tremendous loss in achievement, these remarkable young people are hidden from public view and absent from public policy debates. Instead of being recognized for their excellence and encouraged to strengthen their achievement, high-achieving lower-income students enter what we call the "achievement trap"—educators, policymakers, and the public assume they can fend for themselves when the facts show otherwise. (Wyner et al., 2007, p. 4)

Sometimes a family's low-income situation is temporary, but it may also be a persistent circumstance. It may appear that education is not valued in a particular family; however, the case may be that the parents are very interested in their child's education but are so busy working at lower paying jobs that they have little time to make it to teacher conferences and to find opportunities to communicate with educators. Nonetheless, the child may be exceptional in one or several subject areas in school and should not be overlooked due to the stereotype that gifted children only come from middle- and upper-income families.

# CLUES THAT A CHILD HAS ADVANCED ABILITIES

The first step in developing talent is to recognize advanced ability or the potential for outstanding performance. One clue may be noticing a child reading books that are typically read by older children. A child could be making mathematical connections that are advanced when compared with others in a similar environment. Another indicator of high ability would be noticing an interest that comes close to being a passion area. Still another clue to exceptional potential relates to observing how the child spends time when not in school. It is important to be observant, recognizing that the expression of interests that are typical of older children is another clue of the exceptional potential. The following scenarios describe each of those possibilities.

Simon was a 7-year-old avid reader. Simon was sitting in the back seat of the car, engrossed in a book, when the woman for whom his mother did domestic work noticed his reading habit and book choices. For this lucky boy, a new friendship was formed and his new friend initiated regular trips with Simon to the library at least every other week. Public libraries are full of resources to promote learning, and those resources are available in both print and digital formats.

For Samantha, taking things apart and then putting them back together was a passion. She was interested in how parts fit together as well as how things worked. This interest and preoccupation was not the subject of any class at her elementary school. However, a teacher inquired as to how each of his students spent his or her time when not in school and learned of this curious young girl's passion. Of course, the teacher saw a budding engineer and used every opportunity to steer Samantha in that direction and to stimulate and encourage her learning in math and science. Such an interest would not have surfaced if the teacher had not made an effort to learn about his students' out-of-school interests.

Rafael mentioned to his teacher that he had watched a program on the Discovery Channel about archeologists making new discoveries in and around Rome. Ms. Rader, his teacher, was very surprised at Rafael's interest in ancient history and archeology and shared that information with Mr. Collett, his social studies teacher. That sharing of information led to many conversations between Rafael and Mr. Collett and later to a field trip to the local history museum that further fueled Rafael's interest in history. Passions for learning develop out of interests—interests that may be sparked by a guest speaker, a field trip, a book, a program, a website, a movie, or even a conversation.

Adele seemed fascinated with all things mathematical even though she was only 8 years old. She asked about square roots and negative numbers repeatedly. Her teacher did not expect her to understand the explanation of these concepts, but found that Adele grasped both concepts when offered a fairly brief introduction to them, as well as other advanced concepts in mathematics. No one was sure where this interest was sparked or how Adele grasped mathematical concepts so quickly.

Nonetheless, she did, and that interest was further stimulated as Adele moved to study math with students a couple of grades older than she. When she reached the seventh grade, Adele was encouraged to take the SAT or the ACT as a part of one of the regional talent searches. She did, and the fees for participating in the talent search and registering for an off-level norm-referenced test were waived based on her family's income. A score above the average for high school juniors qualified Adele for the summer program offered by the local university. Each opportunity was made possible by interested educators who made certain that Adele and her family knew about them and also provided information about financial assistance.

In all four situations, individuals served as talent scouts, noticing behaviors that were not typical for a child and his or her age-mates. But things did not stop there. Instead, the adult communicated with another adult and/or took action to further the interest and build on the strength of the child. Having limited family resources should not place limits on the child's potential. Children need idea-mates—others who share their interests. Those others may be children or young people (perhaps older than they are), teachers, or other adults who become the child's mentor.

# EFFECTIVE STRATEGIES

There are many effective strategies to encourage children who are advanced and come from lower income backgrounds. Three strategies—role models, enrichment in school, and Saturday and summer programming—are discussed here; however, there are many more effective strategies to explore.

## ROLE MODELS

Children need role models. It may be that children find role models at the community center, in a church, or in a youth group or club, but they also need to find role models at school. Role models set the standard for how children should act and what they can become. They share with children what they see as appropriate expectations for behavior (including appropriate speech and dress) in a variety of situations. They help children set their sights on goals that stretch them and help them see that goals are worth working to reach. Role models raise expectations for children, sharing possibilities that young people may never have considered because they may have never known anyone who pursued that interest or occupation. Role models can make all the difference in the world to children.

## ENRICHMENT IN SCHOOL

Enriching learning opportunities can be part of the school experience on an ongoing basis. They can be regular curriculum offerings that engage students in learning with hands-on and minds-on learning. They can be science experiments, literacy circles with peers who read at the same challenging level, social studies experiences that engage interest and require high-level thinking, and learning opportunities that thread the arts through the curriculum. Learning needs to pique the interests of children at all possible times—hopefully, on an ongoing basis.

A recent international study (OECD, 2011) found that taking additional courses in science makes a difference for young people from lower income families. "Taking more science courses benefits disadvantaged students even more than it does their more advantaged peers. Therefore, exposing disadvantaged students to science learning at school might help close performance gaps" (OECD, 2011, p. 11).

## SATURDAY AND SUMMER PROGRAMMING

Opportunities are not real opportunities unless the person who would benefit knows about them. It is important that adults inform children of opportunities. They must make sure that young people from lower income families know about financial assistance that can make an opportunity a reality. For example, Saturday and summer programs are offered at various universities. Such programming opportunities are seldom free for participants, but occasionally they are funded by a foundation or a grant. Scholarships based on financial need are often available. Without the help of educators, Saturday and summer programs are out of reach of many young people from lower income families unless educators provide information about how to access such resources and ensure that they make that information known to students and their families. Applications for financial assistance will likely require letters from the parents, the child, and an educator. The counselor, teacher, or principal can work with parents to make sure that the pieces of the application are completed, compiled, and submitted on time.

Why would it be important for a student to participate in a Saturday or summer program?

- Such programs can spark an interest in a content area or topic that may lead to a college major and/or a career. However, that spark may not ignite without opportunities to learn in areas of interest.

- Saturday and summer programs provide an opportunity for young people to be with idea-mates. These intellectual peers may be older or younger, but they all share an interest in a topic. It is important for students to learn that they are not alone in their interests in airplanes or drama and that they can find other idea-mates who are more interested in computer programming than in the current fad in fashion or the television program that is the rage. Kingsolver (2002) described her daughter's summer camp experience with gifted young people, saying it "helped her understand the potential rewards of belonging to a peer group that's more interested in Jane Austen and Shakespeare than Calvin Klein and Tommy Hilfiger" (p. 9).

- If the program is held on a college or university campus, it provides the opportunity for the student to see what a campus is like. If the program is residential, it is a chance to "sample" living in a residence hall and to experience walking on campus in order to preview the college experience. It is easier to set college as a goal if you have comfortable and successful experiences on a campus. Such experiences increase the possibilities that the young person will see college as an attainable goal.

- When the Saturday or summer experience includes young people from various socioeconomic levels, the experience helps to build confidence on the part of students.

Sometimes the first step to begin collaboration between parents of children from lower income families and teachers is to find ways to bring the parents to school—ways that offer a positive experience. If being in school was not an especially good memory for family members, they may not readily accept an invitation to come talk. They may assume that a call from school will have a negative message if that's what they experienced growing up. What they need to experience are good times at school, perhaps when students' work or performances are the focus of the school visit. Finding ways to build positive relationships with parents and families may well begin with opportunities to get them inside the school building and to begin to build a backlog of positive experiences. These positive experiences might include a science or math night at school with lots of activities that focus on ways the family can be involved in these subjects at home. It might be a family reading night, or it might be a family movie night with popcorn for all. These positive experiences may be the first step in creating opportunities for teachers and parents to collaborate with a focus on the child. They may be the conversation starter.

# TIPS FOR COMMUNICATING WITH PARENTS AND FAMILIES FROM LOWER INCOME BACKGROUNDS

The following is a list of tips to help educators communicate with parents and families from lower income backgrounds:

- Establish a positive environment for conversations.
- Be certain to start by commenting on the child's strengths.
- Discuss ways the parents can support the child's interests and learning at home.
- Ask parents if there are any interests the child has that the teacher may not know about and for ideas to help encourage the child at school.
- Establish a goal or goals that will continue the collaboration between the teacher and parents.

# CONCLUDING COMMENTS

Children with gifts and talents come from families in all income levels. In order to encourage the development of their talents and academic abilities, it is imperative to eradicate the myth that gifted children come from only middle- and upper income families. Recognizing gifts and talents as well as their potential marks the first step in talent development. Recognition must be followed by strategies for developing talents to the highest levels possible. Parents and educators must collaborate in order to ensure that talents and abilities continue to advance.

# TOOLS FOR DIGGING DEEPER

Bascomb, N. (2011). *The new cool: A visionary teacher, his FIRST robotics team, and the ultimate battle of smarts.* New York, NY: Crown.

This inspiring story describes a teacher who undertook the challenge of developing STEM (science, technology, engineering, and mathematics) interest and talent with a team for the *FIRST®* LEGO® League.

Carson, B. (1990). *Gifted hands: The Ben Carson story.* Grand Rapids, MI: Zondervan.

Biographies of individuals may be inspirational and can provide quality role models for gifted children. This autobiography tells the tale of a boy living with his mother and brother in inner city Detroit who grows up to be a famous neurosurgeon. His mother worked more than one job and supported Ben's and his brother's achievements in numerous ways—often ways the brothers did not appreciate at the time.

Kitano, M. (2003). Gifted potential and poverty: A call for extraordinary action. *Journal for the Education of the Gifted, 26,* 292–303.

This article examines strategies for increasing representation of low-income children identified for and provided with gifted services.

VanTassel-Baska, J. L. (Ed.). (2010). *Patterns and profiles of promising learners from poverty.* Waco, TX: Prufrock Press.
This resource provides information about various types of diverse learners, all of whom come from poverty backgrounds.

# CHAPTER 4

# Twice-Exceptional Students

People get so caught up in trying to fix the person that they don't see the great diversity and benefits that the person has to bring to the rest of the world.

—Alison Seylor

A child who is twice-exceptional is one who has been identified as having gifts and talents along with one or more disabilities. These children defy the expectations of many educators who do not realize that children can be characterized with dual exceptionalities. If parents or educators do not know about twice-exceptional children, then the chance of a child receiving appropriate educational opportunities diminishes or is nonexistent.

Congress included twice-exceptional children when it established priorities for national activities (Part D) under the Individuals with Disabilities Education Improvement Act (IDEIA) of 2004. In the setting of priorities for funding grants, the law allows the Secretary of Education to give priorities to projects that address the needs of:

- low-achieving students,
- underserved populations,
- children from low-income families,
- limited English proficient children,
- unserved and underserved areas,
- rural or urban areas,
- children whose behavior interferes with their learning and socialization,

- children with reading difficulties,
- children in public charter schools,
- children who are gifted and talented, or
- children with disabilities served by local educational agencies that receive payments under Title VIII of the Elementary and Secondary Education Act of 1965.

Children in each of the categories also can be children who are gifted or advanced. The significance of this listing of priorities is that it is the first time that children who are gifted and talented have been included in any way in the Individuals with Disabilities Education Act.

# DIFFERENT WAYS TO BE TWICE-EXCEPTIONAL: WHAT THIS TERM MEANS

"Twice-exceptionality in the gifted community refers to a student who is gifted academically but also has a disability, or vulnerability, that impedes learning or development in an academic setting" (Assouline, 2010, p. 1). Disabilities or vulnerabilities may manifest themselves in a variety of ways. Disabilities may be sensory or behavioral. They may be physical or learning disabilities. A child may be autistic or have a reading or writing disability. He or she may also have a speech impairment. No matter what the disability, there is great variation among learners who are twice-exceptional, even among children with the same disability. For example, Natalie Estes, a teacher in Warren County, KY, described how different two students with the same disability can be.

As I read about the various characteristics that are specific to one disability, I could visualize my students who are twice-exceptional. I have had two students who have had Asperger's syndrome and were also gifted. They were identified for their general intellect and one also was identified specifically for math. They both had pedantic, seamless speech. And one definitely was all about routine and has problems coping with change. As a result, he became aggressive. This happened more in the regular classroom than during our pull-out sessions. The other student fixated on one topic at a time, so we tried to capitalize on his interests during our GT time. For example, for half the year he was all about theme parks and Walt Disney. He developed a theme park blueprint and developed an iMovie on the life of Walt Disney. (personal communication, October 21, 2011)

Both students were identified as gifted and as having Asperger's syndrome, but at the same time they were unique. To be effective in teaching these two students, the teacher must recognize the strength(s) as well as the disability and accommodate both. For these two students, it was necessary to plan specifically with their strengths and disabilities in mind. Doing so results in students making progress and maximizing their potential.

# CHALLENGES FOR TWICE-EXCEPTIONAL CHILDREN

There are numerous challenges for twice-exceptional children. Once the parents and educators have met the first challenge by recognizing that a child can have a disability and be gifted, only then can they begin to address the strengths and the disabilities. The next challenge is to learn as much as possible about giftedness and also about the specific disability. When educators are not well informed about twice-exceptional children, they may be identified neither as gifted nor as having a disability. Some students may be identified as gifted but struggle because the disability goes unrecognized so accommodations are not made. Still other children are identified with a disability but not as gifted, which often leads to frustration. In order for twice-exceptional children to thrive, strategies to address both their strengths and their disabilities must be implemented. Figure 4 highlights the difficulty of identifying and providing services for twice-exceptional children.

Another challenge is that well-meaning educators may feel a twice-exceptional student is not giving his or her best effort. For example, edu-

| | Yes | No |
|---|---|---|
| Is s/he academically gifted? | ☑ | ☐ |
| Does s/he have a disability impeding her academic progress? | ☑ | ☐ |
| Is s/he, then, twice-exceptional (2e)? | ☑ | ☐ |
| Is identifying and understanding 2e this simple? | ☐ | ☑ |

*Figure 4.* Understanding twice-exceptionality. From "Understanding Twice-Exceptionality," by S. G. Assouline, Summer 2010, *Talent*, p. 1. Copyright 2010 by the Center for Talent Development. Reprinted with permission.

cators may interpret a twice-exceptional child with dysgraphia as lazy rather than seeing a child with a writing disability who needs accommodations in order to thrive in school. Kristi Standiford, a teacher in Daviess County, KY, described her lack of information about twice-exceptional children and how she accommodated the student's gifts and talents once she recognized a twice-exceptional child.

> I had never heard of dysgraphia until this semester. I always thought students with terrible penmanship were just sloppy or lazy. I have a student this semester who early in the semester turned in work that I absolutely could not read. I knew from discussions in class that she was highly intelligent, so I talked to her about her writing. She is the one who told me that she has dysgraphia. It was not documented in her student folder or anywhere. But we have been able to work out alternate ways for her to submit her work or to demonstrate learning. She is a very bright student, but if I had continued to grade her work as I do everyone else's, she would never have passed my class. This student is definitely someone that I would consider 2e [twice-exceptional]. (personal communication, November 18, 2011)

Another challenge is that not all twice-exceptional children will thrive with only one set of accommodations. Instead, general and special education teachers need to collaborate concerning effective strategies. Twice-exceptional children will work with specialists in gifted and special education, and both need to collaborate with the students' classroom teacher(s). Involving both special educators and gifted resource teachers requires intricate scheduling; however, it is worth the effort, as the twice-exceptional children have enhanced opportunities to thrive in school when they work with specialists in gifted and special education. Pooling resources and strategies will be important in creating an individual education plan for twice-exceptional learners. Unless special educators have worked with twice-exceptional children, they may be reluctant to do so, or they may think it is impossible to make arrangements to be serviced by both the special education and the gifted resource teachers. It is even possible that they will think these types of interventions cannot and even need not be done. Of course, such scheduling can be accomplished, and twice-exceptional children are the winners when it happens.

Rebecca Doehlman, a substitute teacher, described a situation in which the special education resource teacher failed to see the possibilities of getting the gifted resource teacher involved and what the consequences were.

> I am a long-term substitute right now in a middle school math class, and there is an autistic student in one of the collaborative classes who is way ahead of the others. He catches on so quickly. I discussed his case with the collaborative teacher, and she was aware of his ability, but she told me they couldn't place him in the accelerated class because he needs to be in a classroom with a collaborative teacher. It breaks my heart to see this. Unfortunately, I don't know if I'll still be there after Thanksgiving, but I'm definitely going to be adjusting instruction to help him while I'm there. He really gets frustrated with the other students' inability to catch on, and the other students get frustrated with him when he answers questions because he goes into detailed explanation of how to solve a problem. (personal communication, November 6, 2011)

Misdiagnosis or misinterpretation of behaviors leads to frustration, whereas accommodating the needs of twice-exceptional children encourages productivity in a classroom. Laura Young, an elementary teacher in Bowling Green, KY, described a twice-exceptional child and strategies that addressed his situation.

> It takes a combination of resources to ensure that twice-exceptional children have opportunities to develop their abilities to the highest level. A classroom teacher needs to capitalize on all resources within the school. In addition to the gifted resource teacher, the special education resource teacher or collaborative teacher, the librarian, and the counselor can offer expertise and support. The librarian can access books and other resources of interest for the children. The counselor can help with motivational issues and assist when underachievement, perfectionism, or other concerns surface. It is key to success that parents and educators consider all of the resources in the school as they plan programming for twice-exceptional children. (personal communication, October 15, 2011)

Behaviors of children who are twice-exceptional mystify some educators and parents. These children may know about some topic in great detail. In class they may correctly answer difficult items and miss easier ones. They may do exceptionally well on material presented orally. They may show advanced ability for some subjects, but be below grade level in others. They may appear not to be trying. The danger is that twice-exceptional children may not be seen as especially capable, as their disability hides their exceptional ability to think at high levels, making them perform as average or below-average learners in the classroom or on their schoolwork. Natalia Estes, an elementary curriculum coordinator in Warren County, KY, described one twice-exceptional child.

> Currently, I have a student who as a fourth grader qualified for GT. She qualified in areas of creativity and general intellect. Her teachers were very shocked, and I was very pleased. She is also twice-exceptional. Since her identification I have observed a difference in her teacher's expectations of her, and as a result, her performance has increased. It was like finding a "diamond in the

rough," and she lives for our pull-out sessions. She is thriving, and I look forward to watching her flourish. (personal communication, November 16, 2011)

A further complication stems from the ways states are interpreting the regulations for identifying students as exceptional children under IDEIA. The formal identification of twice-exceptional learners is difficult for various reasons. One of those reasons is how learning disabilities are identified. Currently, many schools are using a Response to Intervention (RtI) model. Previously, a discrepancy between achievement and potential was used to identify twice-exceptional children for programming; however, in RtI regulations, students are identified for services for a learning disability when the performance falls below that of their fellow students. The challenge with using RtI to identify a child as twice-exceptional is tied to performance that may not be falling below that of their classmates, yet the child's performance does not match his potential for achievement. The strengths may be allowing the child to mask disabilities, or the disabilities may actually mask the strengths.

Twice-exceptional students see the world differently. Before judging them, their behavior, or their likes and dislikes, educators need to get to know them. Understanding their perspective is the key to building a relationship with them and helping them experience success.

# NEGOTIATING THE ROUTE FOR TWICE-EXCEPTIONAL LEARNERS

Weinfeld, Barnes-Robinson, Jeweler, and Shevitz (2006) provided guidance for educators and parents to use to negotiate the challenges presented by a twice-exceptional student (see Figure 5).

Services must match the needs of the twice-exceptional child. They must address the strengths, or the gifted area(s), and the area(s) needing support, or the disability. *The Twice-Exceptional Dilemma* (National Education Association, 2006) described this need for services in both areas:

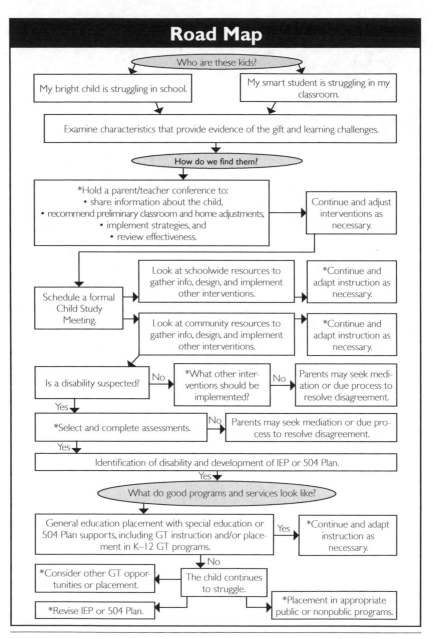

*Figure 5.* Road map. From *Smart Kids With Learning Difficulties: Overcoming Obstacles and Realizing Potential* (p. 8), by R. Weinfeld, L. Barnes-Robinson, S. Jeweler, and B. R. Shevitz, 2006, Waco, TX: Prufrock Press Inc. Copyright 2006 by Prufrock Press Inc. Reprinted with permission.

Just as students with special education needs require services along a continuum, twice-exceptional students require a similar combination of gifted and special education. Rather than satisfaction with at or near grade-level performance, schools should provide special services, programs, and instruction to address both giftedness and disability, thereby teaching the whole child. (p. 3)

Another important consideration when educators are collaborating on behalf of twice-exceptional students is to develop a strategy that will ensure that the child is not characterized by the disability. Working through areas of strength to support the disability and not to have the disability lead the way is important. Identify the strength and concentrate on that area while supporting the needs created by the disability. The focus of the collaboration should be on both the area(s) of strength and the area(s) needing support. Discussions between parents and teachers need to begin by talking about strengths. This does not mean to skip over the areas of disability but rather to place strengths as the focus of the collaboration, so that implementation of a plan will lead with strengths.

One parent of a twice-exceptional learner described what happened with her daughter, Dana, who was a very capable thinker but had a reading disability. The reading disability had gone undetected, as Dana was able to do well enough to perform at an average level. After the diagnosis of the learning disability, Dana was embarrassed and did not want to go to school, as she did not want to be pulled out of her regular class for a special reading class. However, an older friend who had had similar experiences heard about the problem and went out of her way to contact Dana and encouraged her not to be limited by the shortcoming and not to allow the disability to define who she was. She told Dana to see her challenges as just one part of who she was and to focus on her strengths. The young woman advised her to draw pride from her strengths while learning to learn in a different way to overcome her limitations. That advice changed the way Dana approached learning, and she rose above her limitations.

Nobuyuki Tsujii, a Japanese pianist and composer who is also blind, said, "A blind pianist should just enjoy playing the piano, and not think of oneself as being blind" (Rosen, 2010). This quote highlights how important it is to recognize strengths and talents and to be defined by them rather than by a disability. Parents and educators make a huge difference in how twice-exceptional students perceive themselves. It is what they say and do that makes the difference.

# IMPORTANT POINTS FOR HELPING TWICE-EXCEPTIONAL CHILDREN THRIVE

The following are tips for teachers to follow when teaching twice-exceptional students:

- Educators must get to know the child well by observing and listening.
- Parents must be encouraged to share information that will add to the educator's understanding of the child, both his strengths and areas needing support.
- The twice-exceptional student is especially vulnerable to feeling different, and every effort must be made to change those differences into assets.
- Parents and educators must set high expectations for the child, knowing that they must work together in order for the child to thrive in school and beyond.
- The teacher must create a welcoming situation when collaborating with the parents, one that does not overwhelm the parent(s) with a focus on problems.

# TOOLS FOR DIGGING DEEPER

*2e Newsletter*
http://www.2eNewsletter.com
This newsletter on twice-exceptional children and young people is a valuable resource for parents and educators.

*A Chance to Read*
http://www.readingrockets.org/shows/launching/chance
This video from Reading Rockets is one in which Dennis Higgins and Elizabeth Nielsen discuss twice-exceptional children.

Autism Speaks
http://www.autismspeaks.org
This website offers current information and numerous resources related to autism.

NICHCY
http://nichcy.org/laws/idea/copies
The National Dissemination Center for Children with Disabilities (NICHCY) provides up-to-date information about the Individuals with Disabilities Education Act (IDEA) on its website.

Coleman, M. R., & Johnsen, S. K. (Eds.). (2010). *RtI for gifted students.* Waco, TX: Prufrock Press.
This book is a great resource for examining RtI as a model for identifying children who are gifted and talented.

Trail, B. A. (2011). *Twice-exceptional children: Understanding, teaching and counseling gifted students.* Waco, TX: Prufrock Press.
This resource provides practical suggestions for recognizing children who are twice-exceptional and offers strategies for developing their potential.

Webb, J. T., Amend, E. R., Webb, N. E., Goerss, J., Beljan, P., & Olenchak, F. R. (2005). *Misdiagnosis and dual diagnoses of gifted children and adults: ADHD, bipolar, OCD, Asperger's, depression, and other disorders.* Scottsdale, AZ: Great Potential Press.
This book is a resource rich with information about twice-exceptional children and adults.

# CHAPTER 5

# Culturally Diverse Gifted Students

Differences should be celebrated for their contribution to diversity, the very trait that has brought gifted children to our attention. The challenge in educating disadvantaged gifted youth should be to develop potential, not to wish conformity to one model of giftedness with all else being deficient.

—Mary Frazier

Gifted children come from all segments of society, including from diverse cultural backgrounds. "*Culturally different* refers frequently to gifted student from specific ethnic groups including, but not limited to, Hispanics, African Americans, Native Americans, and Asian Americans" (Johnsen, 2011a, p. 25).

It is important that educators understand that being different does not preclude one from being gifted and that educators must be responsive to their needs. Developing talent among all cultural groups is very important in our society, which is becoming increasingly diverse. "Half of all school children will be nonwhite by 2025, and half of the U.S. population will be nonwhite by 2050" (Hodgkinson, 2000, p. 123).

Ford (2011a) described the trends of different student populations in gifted education from 1978–1992 in Table 3. The populations presented in this chart include African Americans, American Indians, Asian Americans, and Hispanic Americans.

Ford (2011a) also provided gifted education demographics for 2000–2006 (see Table 4). Data for 2006 are the most current available from the Office for Civil Rights on gifted education.

## TABLE 3
## TRENDS IN THE REPRESENTATION OF RACIALLY AND CULTURALLY DIFFERENT STUDENTS IN GIFTED EDUCATION PROGRAMS FROM 1978 TO 1992

| Student Population | 1978 | 1980 | 1982 | 1984 | 1992 |
|---|---|---|---|---|---|
| African Americans | 15.7<br>10.3<br>(U = 33%) | 20.1<br>11.1<br>(U = 45%) | 25.8<br>11.0<br>(U = 57%) | 24.5<br>12.9<br>(U = 47%) | 21.1<br>12.0<br>(U = 41%) |
| American Indians | 0.8<br>0.3<br>(U = 62%) | 0.7<br>0.3<br>(U = 57%) | 0.5<br>0.3<br>(U = 40%) | 0.8<br>0.3<br>(U = 62%) | 1.0<br>0.5<br>(U = 50%) |
| Asian Americans | 1.4<br>3.4<br>(O = 59%) | 2.2<br>4.4<br>(O = 50%) | 2.6<br>4.7<br>(O = 45%) | 3.7<br>6.8<br>(O = 46%) | 4.0<br>7.0<br>(O = 43%) |
| Hispanic Americans | 6.8<br>5.15<br>(U = 25%) | 9.0<br>5.4<br>(U = 40%) | 8.6<br>4.0<br>(U = 53%) | 13.2<br>7.2<br>(U = 45%) | 13.7<br>7.9<br>(U = 42%) |

Note. From *Multicultural Gifted Education* (p. xiii), by D. Y. Ford, 2011, Waco, TX: Prufrock Press. Copyright 2011 by Prufrock Press. Reprinted with permission. Percentages are rounded; the top number indicates the percentage of the student population and the middle number represents the percentage of gifted education. The composition index is used, which answers questions such as: What percent of students in special education are Black? In this case, the extent of disproportionality is determined by comparing the composition index to the percent of all students who are Black. Using the composition index, "O" indicates overrepresentation and "U" indicates underrepresentation. Percentage of underrepresentation was calculated using the following: 1 − (percent of gifted education program divided by percent of school district).

# CULTURALLY DIVERSE GIFTED CHILDREN

Culturally diverse gifted and talented children are often underrepresented and underserved in gifted programming. Culture can be defined as "any group of people who share a common structure of values, system of beliefs, set of traditions, language, and/or worldview" (Clark, 2008, p. 324). There are also influencing cultural forces that include "ethnic and racial heritage, religion, gender, age, socioeconomic status, primary

## TABLE 4
## GIFTED EDUCATION DEMOGRAPHICS FOR 2000–2006

| Race/Ethnicity | 2000 | | 2002 | | 2004 | | 2006 | |
|---|---|---|---|---|---|---|---|---|
| | % School District | % Gifted and Talented | % School District | % Gifted and Talented | % School District | % Gifted and Talented | % School District | % Gifted and Talented |
| American Indian/Alaskan Native | 1.16 | .91 | 1.21 | .93 | 1.21 | .93 | 1.24 | .97 |
| Black | 16.99 | 8.23 | 17.16 | 8.43 | 17.16 | 8.43 | 16.99 | 8.99 |
| Hispanic/Latino | 16.13 | 9.54 | 17.80 | 10.41 | 17.80 | 10.41 | 20.41 | 12.79 |
| Asian/Pacific Islander | 4.14 | 7.00 | 4.42 | 7.64 | 4.42 | 7.64 | 4.81 | 9.40 |
| White | 61.58 | 74.24 | 59.42 | 72.59 | 59.42 | 72.69 | 56.42 | 67.69 |
| Total | 100.00 | 100.00 | 100.00 | 100.00 | 100.00 | 100.00 | 100.00 | 100.00 |

*Note.* From *Multicultural Gifted Education* (p. xiii), by D.Y. Ford, 2011, Waco, TX: Prufrock Press. Copyright 2011 by Prufrock Press. Reprinted with permission. Collected from Office for Civil Rights Elementary and Secondary School Data (2002–2008). Data are collected every 2 years and based on the previous 2 years.

language, geographical region, disabilities, and other exceptional conditions" (Clark, 2008, p. 325). Recognizing talent with diverse cultures is an important need in our society.

> Everyone has a culture. No one is born with a culture; instead, the culturalization process begins at birth—culture is learned or acquired as a function of being raised: first, in a family and community and, then, in a school or other social milieu. (Ford, 2011a, p. 38)

*Mind the (Other) Gap!* (Plucker, Burroughs, & Song, 2010) is a report that focuses on the excellence gap in education in the United States. It presents data showing that few young people from the historically underrepresented groups in gifted programming are performing at a level of excellence.

> A convincing body of evidence suggests that an achievement gap exists at higher levels of academic performance. The economically disadvantaged, English Language Learners, and historically underprivileged minorities represent a smaller proportion of students scoring at the highest levels of achievement. (Plucker et al., 2010, p. 28)

All students must have ongoing opportunities to learn at the highest levels. High expectations are vitally important in encouraging young people to achieve at high levels.

# IDENTIFICATION OF GIFTED CULTURALLY DIVERSE CHILDREN

There are certain measures that can be implemented to help identify a greater number of culturally diverse students. These measures can tap the interests, talents, and gifts of children who are linguistically, culturally, and ethnically diverse.

"There is no one best assessment for identifying gifted students;

rather, multiple assessments should be chosen based on the characteristics of the students" (Ryser, 2011, p. 67). Identification protocols should include holistic measures of giftedness rather than relying heavily or even solely on measures of intelligence (Baldwin, 2004). It is also suggested that nonverbal measures of intelligence, such as the Raven's Progressive Matrices Test or the Naglieri Nonverbal Ability Test, be used instead of traditional measures, which rely heavily on verbal abilities (Clark, 2008). Ryser (2011) noted, "Nonverbal measures hold promise for identifying culturally and linguistically diverse students and students from economically disadvantaged backgrounds as gifted. They cannot be the only type of measure used, but should be included as one measure in an assessment battery" (p. 70).

Additional measures can include teacher and parent checklists, which inquire about a child's behavior both at home and school; creativity measures; and portfolios of work representing a student's strengths.

> Practices that appear to be effective in increasing the number of gifted students from special populations in gifted education programming include developing more inclusive definitions, using fair and nontraditional tests, and changing teacher and parent attitudes so that more students are included in the identification process. (Johnsen, 2011a, p. 88)

Preexisting views and assumptions held by teachers can impact culturally diverse students' access and performance in gifted programming. Adjustments or an examination of current assumptions might be made with the following ideas in mind:

- Giftedness expressed in one dimension is just as important as giftedness expressed in another.
- Giftedness can be expressed through a variety of behaviors.
- Giftedness in any area can be a clue to the presence of potential giftedness in another area, or a catalyst for the development of giftedness in another area.
- A total ability profile is crucial in the educational planning for the gifted child.

- Carefully planned subjective assessment techniques can be used effectively in combination with objective assessment techniques.
- Behaviors classified as gifted should be above and beyond the average of a broad spectrum of individuals. (as cited in Baldwin, 2004, p. xxvii)

## SERVICES FOR CULTURALLY DIVERSE GIFTED CHILDREN

Standardized programming can be another impediment when schools and districts impose the same programming for all gifted students regardless of students' strengths or areas of talent. A range of services rather than one gifted program is far more likely to build interest and engage gifted and talented children in learning. Young people are more likely to participate in services when they see value in doing so, and that is most likely to happen when the services match their talents and interests.

Perhaps a sports analogy will highlight the importance of matching services to needs, interests, and readiness. All young people who are athletes are not equally interested in the same sport; some might prefer to play baseball, basketball, or tennis whereas others would rather swim or run track. Yet all are athletes. Another level of diversity becomes evident when individual young people's skills are assessed for readiness or level of skill development in a particular sport. Athletes who play on varsity teams have a higher level of athletic skill than other young people of the same age, yet on the basketball team, for example, the level of skill differs among the athletes for making three-point shots, blocking shots, and completing free throws; consequently, the need for specific coaching differs. If coaches offer one set of experiences (one-sizes-fits-all advice) to prepare all members of the team to play competitively, they will not be nearly as successful as if they tailor feedback or the talent development advice to the individual based on readiness and level of skill development. Just as athletes have interests and skills in various sports, students who are gifted and talented have different interests and propensities in different content areas. Making a match between instruction, interests, and readiness increases motivation to learn at high levels.

Providing appropriate role models and new experiences for young people is important in order to establish personal and professional goals. Roszalyn Akins, director of the BMW (Black Males Working) Academy, a collaborative program of First Bracktown, Inc. and the Fayette County Public School System, described a program that was designed to do just that.

> Our school system has given us the funding to open a program that resembles our BMW Academy. We are so excited. It will be called the Carter G. Woodson Academy for boys. It will be a college prep school where the boys will wear a sport coat every day. Now for the thoughts concerning low-income gifted students. In meeting the needs of gifted students, we provide the three E's. Expectations cause students to respond if you believe in them, and that expectation level can come from teachers or a mentor. Gifted students respond if they believe someone believes in them. Relationship means so much to them. They seek to please those who please them. The second E is exposure. Getting students out of their environment and exposing them to different things helps so much. We believe that we need to expose them to college campuses through visits and summer programs. The third E is experiences. We cover experiences through service-learning projects, community service, and internships. We also work very hard to expose them to positive role models. You cannot be what you don't see. (personal communication, January 12, 2012)

Colleges and universities offer summer and Saturday programs for gifted students. Usually financial assistance is available to ensure that children and young people who qualify will have the opportunity to participate no matter what the income levels of their families. Olszewski-Kubilius (2007) described the following benefits of programming at colleges and universities:

- perceptions of increased social support for learning and achievement due to homogeneous grouping with other gifted students and support from teachers and counselors;

- positive feelings due to being in a learning situation that presents a more appropriate match between the student's intellectual abilities and the challenge or rigor of a course;
- development of study skills as a result of immersion in an intellectually challenging course;
- development of independence and enhancement of general living skills in residential programs because of living away from home on one's own;
- increased knowledge about university programs and college life;
- raising of expectations and aspirations for educational achievement as evidenced by higher educational and career aspirations due to success in a challenging learning environment;
- reinforcement for risk taking as evidenced by seeking other academically challenging environments as a result of extending oneself both intellectually and socially;
- growth in acceptance of others, knowledge of different cultures, and an enhanced worldview as the result of living and socializing with a more diverse group of students; and
- self-testing of abilities due to placement in an intellectually challenging situation and subsequent reevaluations and goal setting that can further a student's progress in attaining excellence. (pp. 19–20)

# GIFTED ENGLISH LANGUAGE LEARNERS

Gifted and talented children who are English language learners are tangential to the discussion of culturally diverse gifted children. Many children who are not from the dominant culture may also be English language learners. Of course, children who come from families in which English is not the first language can be advanced, gifted, or talented (whichever term is used). Often hidden by the lack of ability to communicate easily in the predominant language, students need opportunities to discover and reveal their areas of strength. English language learners are at a disadvantage in school because they are not able to understand, speak, read, and/or write at a level to demonstrate proficiency. Teachers must be looking for clues or behaviors that will provide glimpses, indicators, or hard evidence that English language learners are exceptional thinkers or show exceptional potential in some area(s).

## STRATEGIES FOR FINDING GIFTED ENGLISH LANGUAGE LEARNERS

One way to determine the interests or strengths of students who are English language learners is to communicate using symbols such as mathematical symbols. Being a universal language, math is often an area in which children who are mathematically talented might communicate their talent without the constraints of the English language.

A clue that the children are advanced thinkers is the rate at which they become proficient in the English language. One characteristic of children who are advanced learners relates to the pace of learning. They pick up on the concepts and skills at a more rapid rate than most children of their age. A rapid rate of learning is a strong indication that children may be advanced learners. Such signals should be noted and provide the motivation to differentiate for students in order to help them make continuous progress. If children are able to move along at a more rapid pace than their peers in acquiring language, they deserve opportunities to do so. Differentiating will facilitate learning for all students, including those who are just learning the English language.

An opportunity for an English language learner to shine in school is in art, another non-language-based symbol system. Any visual explanation allows the students to develop and demonstrate their skills at artistic pursuits. Talent in the visual arts can be nurtured as children are working to be proficient in the dominant language. Not all children have exceptional artistic talent, but teachers never know where exceptional abilities will be revealed unless students have opportunities to show what they can visualize and draw or illustrate. Some young people will shine when given opportunities in the arts.

Another example for identifying advanced learners among English language learners would be observing students playing games of logic, such as chess. At a small Kentucky school with quite a few children whose families have recently moved to the United States, a strong chess program is offered. The teacher who taught English language learners thought about teaching chess in his classroom, and when he offered to teach this game of strategy and skill, he discovered a lot of interest. One student became so good at chess that the teacher talked with the principal and the adult volunteer leader of the chess program about the student playing with the students in the afterschool program. When the English language learner played chess against the best chess player in the school, he won. What a perfect demonstration of advanced thinking, and what a wonderful opportunity for the student to feel great about being in school.

It is always a good practice to highlight strengths while working on an area of need. In the case of students with language barriers, the immediate need is to acquire the language in order to be able to learn with other children in the dominant culture. Another example for emphasizing strengths with English language learners came with an extracurricular opportunity in chess. Samuel Hunt, President of the Chess Club at Western Kentucky University, described this opportunity.

> I took two girls from Warren Central High School today to participate in the high school section of the chess tournament. They came in 1st place and 2nd place in their section. They received a lot of compliments about how good their skills were. The positive benefit is that, without our expansion of chess into the county schools this year, we would have never been able to share that experience with those girls or the school. In between rounds, many of the highly rated coaches wanted to come play those girls, and even some of the younger players asked to do so, too. Also, a parent told them what great role models they were for other kids.
>
> Lastly, these girls were telling me about how they don't feel like they fit in since they are from Cuba. The fact that we could meld this very positive, happy day into their living experience while residing here in Bowling Green is icing on the cake. It boosted their confidence. (personal communication, December 8, 2011)

# TIPS FOR COMMUNICATING WITH PARENTS AND FAMILIES OF GIFTED ENGLISH LANGUAGE LEARNERS

If parents and families of English language learners are to support their children in their learning at school, teachers and other school personnel must create opportunities for families to share information about their children. The following ideas are tips for developing such opportunities:

- Create an environment that is comfortable for the parents.
- Find individuals fluent in the language spoken at home to facilitate communication.
- Have newsletters and notes to parents translated into the language spoken at home.
- Focus on the advantages to their child of participating in special classes, programming, or opportunities.

# CONCLUDING THOUGHTS

The need to nurture the talents and interests of culturally diverse gifted children is imperative. Students with gifts and talents must be matched to services that will allow them to access opportunities within school as well as in postsecondary education. Fair and equal access to programming and relevant and rigorous opportunities to learn must characterize the elementary, middle, and high school experiences for all children, including those who are culturally diverse. To accomplish these goals, it is necessary to get rid of myths that get in the way of seeing all children—including culturally diverse students—as having potential.

# TOOLS FOR DIGGING DEEPER

Adams, C. M., & Boswell, C. (2012). *Effective program practices for underserved gifted students*. Waco, TX: Prufrock Press.
This book examines strategies that work in developing the potential of diverse gifted learners.

Davis, J. L. (2010). *Bright, talented, & Black: A guide for families of African American gifted learners*. Scottsdale, AZ: Great Potential Press.
This book provides practical advice for families of gifted African American children. The strategies suggested will guide teachers as well.

Grantham, T., & Ford. D. Y. (2003). Providing access for culturally diverse gifted students: From deficit thinking to dynamic thinking. *Theory Into Practice, 42,* 217–225.
This article encourages educators to use dynamic thinking as they educate children from culturally diverse backgrounds, making sure to develop their talents.

Stambaugh, T., & Chandler, K. L. (2012). *Effective curriculum for underserved gifted students*. Waco, TX: Prufrock Press.
This book provides numerous examples of curriculum modifications that are appropriate for developing the potential of culturally diverse learners.

# CHAPTER 6

# Gifted Students Who Are Limited by a Ceiling on Learning

I have come to a frightening conclusion.
I am the decisive element in the classroom.
It is my personal approach that creates the climate.
It is my daily mood that makes the weather.
As a teacher I possess tremendous power to make a child's life miserable or joyous.
I can be a tool of torture or an instrument of inspiration.
I can humiliate or humor, hurt or heal.
In all situations, it is my response that decides whether a crisis
will be escalated or de-escalated, and a child humanized or de-humanized.
—Haim Ginott

A common problem in schools is the belief that many educators have that gifted children "will make it on their own." Quite the contrary, children with gifts and talents, including those from diverse backgrounds, need to be taught and guided to develop their potential. "Making it on their own" implies that teachers will concentrate on children who are working below or on grade level, and that they will leave the advanced or high-ability children to fend for themselves. Obviously, that is not the strategy that is used to develop athletic ability, and it is not a strategy that is successful in developing the gifts and talents of students.

Do not underestimate the power you have as a teacher to influence a child's life. In a climate of high-stakes testing and the adherence to scripted curriculum, the humanness of the profession has been overrun with a mechanistic approach to instruction. However, if one examines the biographies and memoirs of successful and eminent people, many of these individuals will identify a teacher as one of the influential persons in their lives. These teachers provided guidance, encouragement, and opportunities for them as children to test new ideas, see their thinking as having no limits, and work toward a goal that was bigger than they had imagined. Influential teachers can be especially important in urban and rural communities, where the environment may lack resources and human capital. The following individuals have accomplished exceptional achievements, and years after leaving school, still identified a teacher who recognized and encouraged their potential.

Antwone Fisher, an award-winning film and literary writer, was born in a Cleveland, OH, prison to a teenage mother and was raised in the foster care system. During his years in foster care, he suffered horrible abuse at the hands of his foster mother. School seemed like an extension of his situation at home, where kids were arranged according to whether they were "better" or "bad," until Antwone entered Mrs. Profit's class for grades 4–6. Those 3 years were instrumental in building Antwone's self-esteem and self-confidence. Mrs. Profit arranged for field trips to places and events the children from this working-class neighborhood would not have typically seen. Rather than deducing what each child was capable of based on the circumstances from which he or she came, Mrs. Profit refrained from what we now call *deficit thinking* (Grantham & Ford, 2003), and treated each child as a unique individual with potential and promise. Fisher recounted in his memoir, *Finding Fish* (Fisher & Rivas, 2001), "She treats everyone as special, me included. . . . She gives each of us the same chance to do well" (p. 123).

Walter Dean Myers, respected and noted author of young adult literature, grew up in Harlem, the adopted son of a biracial couple during the 1950s. In school he had a reputation for fighting with his teachers until he reached the sixth grade and Mr. Irwin Lasher. Mr. Lasher surmised that Walter was a bright kid, despite an ongoing problem with his speech, and expected him to live up to his potential. Myers (2001) remembered,

Mr. Lasher did two important things that year. The first was that he took me out of class one day per week and put me in speech therapy for the entire day. The second thing he did was to convince me that my good reading ability and good test scores made me special. (p. 58)

Myers is what we would today call twice-exceptional, bright with some type of disability that impeded his learning. He would go on to attend the prestigious Stuyvesant High School, a public school focused on math and science in New York City. With his love of reading, writing, and philosophy, this perhaps was not the best match for his abilities or interests. After struggling for the first time in his school career due to the unfamiliar demanding curriculum, Myers (2001) thought about dropping out prior to his senior year: "If it hadn't been for English, I would have never returned to 15th Street. The teacher, a dark-haired, intense woman, also ran the Creative Writing workshop" (p. 143). She encouraged him to expand his reading choices and helped him to make a "connection between my reading and writing process" (Myers, 2001, p. 144). Although Myers did not graduate from high school, his time in this English class left an indelible impression on him—he never gave up on his writing.

Homer Hickam, author of the book *Rocket Boys*, grew up in the coal-mining town of Coalwood, WV. Most boys in this town were expected to grow up and work in the coal mines just as their fathers had before them. In rural communities such as these, careers can often revolve around one industry. Hickam's interest in rockets grew from the Soviet rocket launch, Sputnik I. Miss Riley, his high school science teacher, fostered his and his friends' interest in rocketry, which would eventually lead to their entering the National Science Fair. From this exposure, he received college scholarship offers and eventually enrolled at Virginia Tech. Miss Riley's support was integral in the continual pursuit of rocketry; his father was not initially supportive of this interest. During the trial-and-error phase of their rocket building, Homer looked to Miss Riley for approval and assistance (Hickam, 1998).

Looking past their students' circumstances, these teachers became identifiers, supporters, and encouragers of special talents or abilities.

Teachers may not immediately see the impact of their influence, but recognizing potential may be enough to keep a student on a persistent road. Children who attend school in more contemporary times face different challenges than the previous examples, but nonetheless are in need of special teachers who understand gifted children's unique learning needs and are willing to intercede on their behalf. Two current examples are included below.

Sabrina, a second grader, has recently been identified as gifted by a private psychologist. The school district she currently attends provides one hour of pull-out gifted services a week. She attends public school in a suburban district where differentiation is highly touted as a common classroom practice in the district. There are 26 students in Sabrina's class who are at various ability levels. Sabrina reads at a sixth-grade level. Despite the district's commitment to differentiation, Sabrina's teacher spends the majority of her time working with her students who are struggling; thus, Sabrina is content to read her library books and writes her own stories in class and causes little trouble for the teacher. She rarely has homework, as she easily finishes assignments during class. Sabrina's teacher figures that she receives gifted services already and perceives the other students' academic needs to be more urgent. Due to Sabrina's observed self-sufficiency, the teacher leaves her to her own devices much of the school day.

Cedric is a fifth grader in an elementary school in an urban school district. This is his first year at this school and the second year in a row his school has been identified as low performing by the state—with a takeover by the state being threatened. Many of his classmates read below grade level and struggle with other content areas as well. The district and school administration are focused on raising test scores and escaping the low-performing list. Classrooms are being monitored to ensure that the prescribed curriculum is being followed; there is no straying from scripted curriculum, regardless of children's readiness levels. No one is moving on until the curriculum guide says so. Cedric has been ready to move on since the first day of school. He languishes in a classroom that is working on math concepts that he understood in second grade. There are no gifted services at Cedric's school, so it is up to the regular classroom teacher to make sure that his learning needs are being met.

No Child Left Behind (NCLB) and the high-stakes testing move-ment (it is too soon to know the implications of President Obama's less-ening of NCLB requirements) have placed many teachers in the same position as Cedric's teacher of having to follow a lock-step or scripted curriculum with little variation for learners of different abilities. Loveless, Farkas, and Duffet (2008) reported that "more than three in four (77%) agree that getting underachieving students to reach 'proficiency' has become so important that the needs of advanced students take a back seat" (p. 61). In addition, there are no or limited opportunities for profes-sional development on how to work with gifted or high-ability students (Loveless et al., 2008).

With the pressure to meet testing requirements and leave the low-performing list, school administrators and teachers rely on strategies that they perceive as providing continuity and consistency regardless of their appropriateness for learners of different ability. For kids like Cedric, this makes school a rather boring and frustrating place to spend the major-ity of the day. Unlike Sabrina, Cedric cannot even keep himself engaged by reading a library book on his own ability level. He must follow along with the rest of his classmates. This boredom has turned into disrup-tion on several occasions, including trips to the principal's office. Cedric is at risk for underachievement. If his classroom environment does not change, the odds greatly increase that he will become an underachiever. However, there are strategies that teachers and parents can employ both separately and in tandem.

Cedric's single father, Alvin, is the caregiver for both Cedric and his younger sister; he works long hours to provide for his children. Despite having great interest in his son's education, Alvin does not always have the time or financial resources to spend with Cedric and his sister and relies on extended family to fill in the gaps. How can teachers and parents (and in this case extended family) work together to address Cedric's learning and behavioral needs? There are many opportunities in communities that are either free or low cost to children and their families, including com-munity centers, libraries, Boys and Girls Clubs of America, and muse-ums. Based on Cedric's interests, a little research, and input from parents to help find a good match, opportunities can be identified that represent a broad spectrum of opportunities based on locale, cost, and interest.

Some educators erroneously believe that gifted children can make it on their own. They finish work ahead of time with very little or no direction from the teacher. However, who is going to facilitate their learning when they are ready to move on to something new? Not offering gifted children work that is commensurate with their abilities can cause a loss of motivation or interest in school. Research also indicates that children who are not challenged may not be able to maintain their current level of brain development.

Sabrina is lucky that she attends a school with a gifted program regardless of the type or number of services offered. There is a gifted teacher on campus who can work cooperatively with Sabrina's regular classroom teacher to provide augmented curriculum that better meets her learning needs.

The school day presents a finite amount of time during which a teacher can influence a child's life. Grantham and Ford (2003) suggested moving from deficit to dynamic thinking. Rather than focusing on what the child lacks, teachers should recognize and work to build on his or her strengths. Additionally, community resources that were mentioned earlier can be accessed to help supplement the learning of children like Sabrina and Cedric.

# DYNAMIC THINKING

Teachers must explore their own perceptions of groups other than themselves. For those students who come from diverse backgrounds, it is important for educators to familiarize themselves with their cultural backgrounds. Education about the needs of gifted and talented students is equally important. Recognizing the academic, social, and emotional characteristics of gifted students from a range of diverse cultural and socioeconomic backgrounds will help teachers identify students for recommendation to gifted programming, arrange appropriate curricular experiences in the classroom, and communicate other possible opportunities outside of school to parents and caregivers. Cultivating relationships and establishing good communication with families are equally important in order to advocate for gifted children and provide appropriate opportunities for learning (Grantham & Ford, 2003).

# COMMUNITY RESOURCES

Community resources can supplement learning and help those children who are limited by the curriculum in the classroom. These resources are often low cost or free, enabling budget-challenged schools and teachers to extend their curricula beyond the school walls.

## COMMUNITY CENTERS AND LIBRARIES

Community centers and libraries can offer quality programming in a variety of subjects and for an array of ability levels. Community centers are excellent resources for activities that include courses in sports, technical courses, and the arts. Libraries also hold a wealth of resources. Apart from providing children like Cedric and Sabrina with books at their reading level, libraries often offer programming and speakers that are free of charge. Some even have mobile book borrowing bus that will bring the books to areas where library access is limited. Local libraries also have brick and mortar resources, as well as many online databases that include books, musical recordings, and pictures. Library cards are free, as are many of the programs and services that libraries offer. These programs and services include children's story times for a variety of age groups, computer classes, book clubs, chess classes, genealogy workshops, summer reading programs, and arts and crafts.

## SUMMER PROGRAMS

Summer programs for gifted children have become more commonplace over the past several decades and are likely to increase due to a disconnect between in-school offerings and student need. Universities and colleges typically offer these programs. Often, "these programs provide a level of challenge and a pace of learning that are more suitable to the intellectual capabilities of gifted students and are very different from what they encounter in school" (Olszewski-Kubilius, 2007, p. 13).

These environments also allow students such as Cedric and Sabrina to be around other children of similar abilities or interests. The social relationships with other children and adults developed during this type of programming are also important for students at risk for not reaching their potential, many of whom eventually return for further summer programming (Johnsen, Feuerbacher, & Witte, 2007). For a listing of summer programs across the United States, see the Resources section of this book. In this type of environment, students have the opportunity to explore a topic of interest in greater depth, experience accelerated content, or be exposed to curriculum not normally taught in school.

## COMPETITIONS

Competitions also present a unique opportunity for children to exercise and display their talents at a high level. These competitions can occur in or outside of school. Even though concerns have been raised regarding equitable access to competitions, especially when considering the cost related to entry, travel, and materials, with thoughtful implementation competitions can benefit children greatly (Riley & Karnes, 2007). Competitions also represent an opportunity for parents, teachers, and schools to work together. Parents and other caregivers can provide support at home while teachers and schools can promote competitions that complement the curriculum at school that sometimes are "isolated, stand-alone experiences, inappropriate for achieving excellence" (Riley & Karnes, 2007, p. 163). Learning opportunities can be greatly enhanced through competitions, especially in schools like Cedric's where classroom curricula is strictly limited. Things to keep in mind in order to promote excellence and equity through the use of competitions include (Riley & Karnes, 2007) the need to:

- develop selection criteria with a connection between competition goals and a system for identification,
- build financial support and human capital both in the school and community,
- recognize all competitors, and
- offer a broad spectrum of competition opportunities including but not limited to those in the arts, sports, and academics.

The Resources section of this book includes a host of competitions for a wide variety of interests.

## MENTORING

Teachers often recognize a keen interest that a child possesses. If a teacher has limited knowledge of a subject or content area, he or she can help by assisting in finding a child a mentor. Parental support is also integral in this process. Together parents and teachers can help to find the appropriate match between child and mentor. Typically this relationship is built around a particular goal or project (Davidson Institute for Talent Development, 2006).

Mentoring programs or mentors in the community can serve as extensions of certain content areas that may interest children. Mentors can also play a pivotal role in students' lives, particularly those who have a deep passion or interest in a particular subject area. These mentoring relationships can be formal or informal in nature. For a child with a passion, consider online mentoring where experts in various fields exchange e-mails with their mentees regarding their field of work.

There are several organizations that can help facilitate in research and finding an appropriate mentor. These include MENTOR: The National Mentoring Partnership (http://www.mentoring.org), iMentor (http://www.imentor.org), and The Mentoring Group (http://www.mentoringgroup.com). If a local mentor is not available, there are organizations such as The International Telementoring Program (http://www.telementor.org). Mentoring organizations help to build structured one-to-one relationships, cultivate kind and caring relationships, promote individuals to satisfy their fullest potential, and help others in the community to become more active (MENTOR, n.d.). Types of mentoring can include conventional mentoring (one adult to one young person), group mentoring (one adult working with up to four young people), team mentoring (several adults working with small groups of kids), peer mentoring (young people mentoring each other), and e-mentoring (mentoring conducted over the Internet and e-mail). Mentoring locations also can vary, such as the mentor's workplace, at school, a place in the community, or virtually (MENTOR, n.d.). Mentoring can also take place in less formal ways. Many elementary schools have reading friends or math buddy programs. Typically, these programs are set up for struggling learners. Instead, for diverse gifted students, reading friends or math buddies could be matched for their advanced abilities or interests.

## DISTANCE LEARNING

Distance learning has been commonplace in American schooling for the past 200 years. The earliest distance learning programs relied on the postal service as items were mailed back and forth between teacher and student. Today with the Internet, personal computers, and devices such as the iPad or smartphones, learning can take place at a much faster pace nearly anywhere. Children like Cedric are in need of a curriculum beyond what is in his classroom as well as appropriate curriculum within the classroom. However, there are certain factors to consider before embarking on a distance-learning program. Students must be able to take the initiative for their own learning and must have the time to complete the assignments, and typically there is some fee involved (although schools have been known to pay the fees rather than hire a full-time dedicated teacher). There are other questions to consider:

- Is the program accredited or attached to some valid educational agency, and will the course count toward high school or college credit (and will the high school or university accept the credit)?
- Is the program appropriate for gifted or advanced learners?
- Is there a particular sequence or pace to which the student must adhere (Adams & Olszewski-Kubilius, 2007)?

# CONCLUDING COMMENTS

A teacher's influence and support can make all the difference for some students like Cedric and Sabrina. Whether hemmed in by the curricula or by their own views on the ability of gifted children to make it on their own, teachers need to recognize the depth of their influence for better or worse. Antwone Fisher, Walter Dean Meyer, and Homer Hickam are just a few examples of how a teacher's influence changed the course of these individuals' lives. Regardless of the students' home circumstances, socioeconomic status, and race, their teachers focused on their dynamic qualities rather than their deficits. Teachers of students like Cedric and Sabrina can do the same through accessing resources to meet their learning needs and fundamentally changing the way in which they serve their most able students.

# TOOLS FOR DIGGING DEEPER

Hoagies' Gifted: Mentors for Gifted Students
http://www.hoagiesgifted.org/mentors.htm
This website provides multiple resources related to mentoring.

Unwrapping the Gifted Blog
http://blogs.edweek.org/teachers/unwrapping_the_gifted
Tamara Fisher writes for *Education Week*. She covers various topics related to children with gifts and talents.

McCollister, K., & Sayler, M. F. (2010). Lift the ceiling: Increase rigor with critical thinking skills. *Gifted Child Today, 33*(1), 41–47.
This articles highlights strategies for enhancing critical thinking.

# CHAPTER 7

# Stepping Up: Teacher Tips to Stop Bullying[1]

Life is a fight, but not everyone's a fighter. Otherwise, bullies would be an endangered species.

—Andrew Vachss

Most bullying happens because of lack of supervision by caring adults and a lack of sufficient education in diversity and appreciation of all groups of students. This lack of supervision and rise in bullying are especially noticeable in gifted populations. Television, movies, and the media overflow with "funny" stories about "nerds" and "geeks." Because many students who are gifted also are extra sensitive, some gifted boys are labeled "gay" at an early age, leaving children as young as 10 years old to fight on two battlefronts. Educators have created a long list of "no-no's" when it comes to words that are unacceptable in schools. Words have degraded groups for centuries, but the words that humiliate gifted students are still considered okay or tolerated by some educators.

Teachers, principals, and staff often feel as if the real or even perceived harm to a bully victim is "no big deal" because their empathy for certain types of attacks is still very low. Some educators may feel that students such as gifted children who exhibit contrary-to-norm personalities and characteristics might deserve to be bullied because it will teach them how to act "normal."

---

1    This chapter was contributed by Brad Tassell and Janet Hagemeyer Tassell.

As populations become more diverse in language, culture, and race, it is even more important that *all* educators develop the mindset that they must play a minute-by-minute active role in stopping bullying, teaching appreciation, and being a role model—a sense that everybody belongs and no one is to be left out. All educators and parents must make the effort to abstain from marginalizing the pain of others because of misconceptions and the misunderstanding of cultural and other areas of diversity. In addition, educators must change their collective thinking about gifted populations and the harmful effects bullying has on them. Educators can no longer shrug off bullying against gifted students because they are "bringing it on themselves."

## WHAT IS BULLYING?

The initial problem faced in many schools and society is that there is not a clear definition of bullying or the definition is not understood or used in its correct form. Olweus (1993) defined bullying as, "A person is bullied when he or she is exposed, repeatedly and over time, to negative actions on the part of one or more other persons, and he or she has difficulty defending himself or herself" (p. 9).

Bullying is not only hurting someone mentally, physically, or emotionally repeatedly and over time, but it is also an effort to break that person down to a point so he or she feels trapped. A person who is bullied can feel terrorized. This situation can be especially threatening to diverse populations of children who already feel very different and out of their cultural comfort zone. Students with limited English skills, but with high potential for intuition or creativity, may not even know how to ask for help if they are being bullied, yet they are acutely aware the attacks are menacing and not humorous. Gifted students struggling with gender or sexual identity issues may feel that they are wrong for their feelings and that the bullying is justified because of negative messages and homophobic rhetoric they are exposed to from adults, churches, institutions, and societal stereotypes. Gifted preteen boys are especially vulnerable because they are very aware when they do not fit stereotypical male roles. This awareness often consumes them with worry, fear, and even guilt that they have a defect of some sort, so bullying situations are exacerbated by the victim constantly dwelling on them. This constant pondering about negative situations can create a loop of despair that high-potential students feel they have no way out and no one can help.

# TAKE THE PULSE OF THE SCHOOL

Survey tools can be used with students to find out about their attitudes regarding bullying and other concerns, from ideas about diversity to concerns about being different. Technology helps in this respect. Sites such as SurveyMonkey (http://www.surveymonkey.com) provide a fast and easy way for schools, administrators, and teachers to take the pulse of what is going on in a school by creating and administering surveys.

Bullying surveys can be distributed to students at the beginning of the school year and should include both specific and open-ended prompts and questions such as:

- Rate the severity of bullying in the school from 1–10.
- In what areas in the school does most bullying occur?
- Is there anyone you know who is bullying others?
- Is there anyone you know who bullying is hurting?

Educators may also ask a wide range of questions about attitudes toward high ability, divergent groups, and disabilities. One middle school in Kentucky gave out a bullying survey and discovered that the same bathroom and names came up again and again as the biggest bullying problems in the school. These data are able to shape protocols, direct resources, and integrate helpful interventions. They may also guide curriculum when misconceptions about diverse populations are widespread.

# THE INFORMAL CAMPUS

In a 10-year study of the Columbine high school shooting, researchers found that schools that have minimized violence, foiled attacks, and lessened bullying have an informal respectful contact between staff and students (Toppo & Elias, 2009). It was noted that if one visited these schools during lunch, he or she would notice that almost every cafeteria table had a teacher interacting and visiting with the students (Toppo & Elias, 2009).

When caring, respectful supervision is highly visible in the school setting, bullying has a more difficult time taking root. How difficult would it be for a group or a student at lunch to harass a girl because of her weight or tell racist jokes in front of three new Hispanic students when the teacher was sitting at the same table? How many students would feel terrorized on the playground if the monitors continuously moved around to all areas instead of sitting in a group at a picnic table waiting for something to happen?

# STORIES FROM THE PLAYGROUND: YOU'RE NOT THAT HURT

A fourth-grade girl was pushed down while playing soccer on the playground and scraped her knee badly enough to bleed. She asked between growing sobs for a student to please get a teacher for help. The message from the five teachers sitting 100 yards away was, "Tell her to walk over here so we can look at it." Stories like this one are endless. In Florida, a larger boy held a smaller boy in a headlock, and as he slapped his head with an open hand, he yelled, "That enough?" Within a few hundred feet was a group of six educators standing in a closed circle chatting. There wasn't even a hint of fear from the terrorizing boy that anyone would come to the aid of his victim. When this incident was brought with concern to the counselor, the response was, with a shrug, "Yep, that sounds familiar."

Teachers may say that students are often exaggerating their pain or fear of being victimized. The problem is that perceived fear is as strong as actual fear, and students can feel terrorized in situations that adults would see as no real threat. Gifted students often get fixated on certain issues (e.g., being too fat, being too poor, not having the right brand of clothing). This focus can influence teachers' marginalization of students' pain even further because they hear about it all the time and are slower to help when bullying is married to those issues. The educator may be correct in many cases about the severity of harm (or lack thereof), but the long-term effects due to lack of intervention are not worth the risk. Simple solution-focused behavioral interventions called "scaling," where students rate their distress level from 1–10 and are then asked how they can bring that level down a point or two, can make a huge difference (Sklare, 2005). The student feels that an authority is paying attention to his or her needs, and he or she is given a chance to problem solve independent solutions. This type of intervention can gauge students' level of fear or frustration, and can be used to help refer them to services should it be very high, even if an educator believes that the threat is low.

# A LESSON FROM THE LUNCHROOM: HE'S EATING WHAT?

Educators, parents, and administrators can learn a great deal about the pulse of the school at the lunch table. Below one parent relates a particular instance while eating lunch with a group of third-grade students.

At the lunch table, two students were excited to tell a story about another student. Wes was gifted and different. He was sensitive and had many allergies, which caused him to wipe his nose with his sleeve often. The two boys were eager to tell what they had just learned about Wes, and they couldn't wait to pass around the information. They told that Wes was always wiping his nose, and that he had started to take feces out of the toilet with his hands and rub it on the bathroom walls. They also said Wes was rubbing it on his face. They told this story with great enthusiasm, energy, and believability. Their plan was to tell this story to everybody in the school, and the parent was the first to hear of their story. How far would this story have gone to destroying many years of Wes's life had this parent not heard it first? How many stories a day could be circumvented with proper supervision available?

The story did not go farther than the table that day because of the relationship the parent had created with this third-grade class. They felt comfortable enough around the parent to speak openly about their lives and feelings and knew that he would listen, and they also knew he would take the time to teach them right and wrong in a caring, unbiased way. These boys did not dislike Wes. They had made what they felt was a funny leap of exaggeration from wiping a nose on a sleeve to a much more fun and interesting tale of toilet humor. They could only see how fun and funny it would be to spread such a story. They could not see that such things can grow to destroy the self-esteem of the person who is being targeted. The parent explained this to them at the lunch table. He was also able to enlist the teachers to help by having a class discussion about how destructive rumors can be. The boys learned at the table, before any pain or consequences, about appropriate humor. They appreciated that, too, because they had no idea how much trouble they could have gotten into if it was found out, later, they had started these rumors in a zero-tolerance school atmosphere. When teachers—and parents—create this kind of informal relationship with their students, even at the lunch table, they can catch a problem before it becomes a tragedy (Toppo & Elias, 2009).

The playground, the hallways, the locker room, the cafeteria, and the classroom are all places where no students should be left to their own devices for extended periods of time. It takes a mindset that believes there is always benefit and enjoyment in student/teacher interaction and engagement. Students feel more secure when they know they have access to help and supervision at any time. Those feeling inclined to bully will be less apt to take the chance when the likelihood is great they will be noticed and corrected. Schools might create a formal, written supervision plan with adults assigned by name to areas at specific times and locations (Trump, 2011).

# TEACHER TIP: DON'T BE
# A BULLY YOURSELF

Some kids will just rub teachers the wrong way, and teachers will have personality conflicts with certain students. Many teachers have a tendency, through their defensiveness, to put up a battle shield every time they have to deal with certain students. This also happens when they are uncomfortable around students and people who are different from them in race, culture, economic status, gender, sexual orientation, or disability. The issues are even more complex with these groups when they want to make sure they are sensitive to their differences, or are intimidated by them. This situation is most evident with gifted students who exhibit advanced knowledge in many areas, but are immature, have little tact, or feel they are superior. Educators are often harder on them with verbal corrections and are more apt to discipline them because they feel challenged and defensive (Clark, 2008).

In other cases, teachers are hyper-aware that they might lack understanding of culture or disability, and in an attempt not to be wrong in their intervention, they decide to do nothing. Educators often ignore bullying because they fear trying to help will end up reflecting badly on them.

The first step for educators is to recognize their biases and make sure they can put them aside in order not to fall victim to creating a "trickle down" effect (Dubin, 2007). If the teacher does not serve as an intentional positive role model, he or she may lead students down an unintentional path where bullying is perceived as acceptable. It is hard for teachers to admit when they are prejudiced against a group or orientation. No matter if teachers' objections are racially motivated, because of religious grounds, or personality-basis driven, they have no place in the school. Once any other student is aware of the teacher's negative opinion, bullying is seen as appropriate and even warranted. Educators may show their bias in both subtle and overt ways such as using inappropriate terminology or punishing students from certain groups at a more frequent and harsher rate.

In many cases, educators might not even realize they are being inappropriate because some terms have become colloquial. One example is a teacher who was using the term "Dead Indians" to describe the empty drink boxes he was picking up after as class party. Terms that were used 50 years ago are very hurtful to Native Americans and others today even if the educator does not understand their use or they are not used maliciously. Teachers can also misunderstand the use of humor and sarcasm, and a specific example concerns a male coach who joked, "Here comes ugly!" to a fifth-grade girl because she always wore her hair in a ponytail. He believed he was connecting with her using humor, but he misunderstood the difference in perceptions between males and females, especially at the age when puberty begins. Because he and most boys would never care about being called ugly, he believed young girls would have the same perception. Young girls can be devastated when male authority figures belittle their looks or weight even when they do not show such reactions in an overt manner. Add this to the millions of young girls without a male role model at home, and the consequences can be long ranging.

Consider the following when approaching the variety of sensitive scenarios regarding preventing or diffusing bullying:

- using insensitive terminology for LGBTQ (lesbian, gay, bisexual, transgender, and questioning) students;
- characterizing any religion or group as terrorists or wrong in their beliefs;
- referring to socioeconomic status or race as a reason for crime or violence; and
- avoiding calling on and making remarks about gifted students in the classroom because they always have their hands up or are "know it alls."

This is a partial list, but the main point is that all educators must have knowledge of any type of diversity in the classroom. This knowledge also means teaching appreciation for differences well and above the concept of tolerance. Many educators are afraid of different groups because of their lack of familiarity with a particular group. Teachers should seek out opportunities to learn about others' lives, attend festivals of other cultures, go to workshops given on LGBTQ issues, search the Internet for blogs pertaining to religious traditions from a variety of faiths, read books on the nature of gifted children and other special educational groups, and do whatever they need to do to see the value in every student, removing their biases.

# A STORY FROM THE FIELD: CHARLIE BROWN

Recently a third-grade class had its Halloween celebration. The teacher was busy with other things, so as a special treat she showed the

1966 Peanuts film, *It's the Great Pumpkin, Charlie Brown*. The themes of 1966 and the themes of today are very different as the Peanuts gang assaulted, bullied, and belittled one another. Even adults were cruel to children. The film ended without a word from the educator about the movie except that it was time for candy and games. What a great place for discussion about the themes presented, the characters' reactions, and how we should live our lives in comparison. This is not to advocate that schools stop showing a film like *It's the Great Pumpkin, Charlie Brown*. It is just the opposite. Even age-appropriate controversial films and books should be presented as long as the class discusses what is right and wrong about all aspects of the media and literature.

This same school read a beautiful award-winning novel by Lois Lowry, *Number the Stars*, and added projects like researching Denmark's history during WWII, creating a multimedia technology presentation, and discussing the characters' motivations and actions from a first-person perspective. The effect on the students was increased empathy and understanding. Every source of media brought into the classroom can be a learning opportunity. A film like *It's the Great Pumpkin, Charlie Brown* is as good a tool as *Number the Stars* in teaching children about bullying, empathy, appropriate humor, conflict resolution, and tolerance, but it must be used as an educational tool. One main bullying theme that can be discussed after a showing of *It's the Great Pumpkin, Charlie Brown* is: How can bullying be funny in a movie, but not funny in real life? The short answer is everything that happens in a classroom is a chance for learning about tolerance and, more importantly, appreciation.

# HONOR CODE

Every school should have a bullying and behavior policy that is written and presented to students and parents at the beginning of the year. The rules for conduct and steps that will be taken when bullying occurs should be outlined. The honor code also needs to outline what respect for others looks like. Every student and parent should be encouraged to sign this code.

Here is a sample of a Bully-Free Declaration adapted from Dubin's (2007) work:

> We the students, teachers, and parents of _____
> school, declare that all members of the community are valuable
> citizens. We affirm that no student will ever be teased or bul-
> lied with an intention to cause harm. We agree that students
> who choose to act contrary to this policy should be subjected
> to consequences for their actions. It is important to stand up
> for the people who have been bullied and to let those who bully
> know that what he or she is doing is unacceptable. It is in the
> _____ tradition that we affirm these principles
> of inclusion and acceptance for every student, teacher, or mem-
> ber of our community. (p. 128)

In addition, here is a sample contract for parents to be given on first day of school:

> Dear Parents and/or Legal Guardians,
>     Please read and review the Bully-Free Declaration with your
> child. Below you will see a contract that we are asking students
> and parents to sign. Discuss the contract and the importance of
> bullying prevention with your son or daughter before he or she
> returns to school with signed contract tomorrow.
>
>     I_____ agree that I will
> abide by the principles and policies set forth in the Bully-Free
> Declaration. If I don't abide by then, I agree to accept the conse-
> quences for my actions. (Dubin, 2007, pp. 128–129)

# CONCLUDING COMMENTS

Stopping bullying is as much about awareness and supervision as it is about understanding the mindset of those who can find enjoyment through others' pain. Schools already have the tools they need to take the bite out of the bully's bark by trading in the drama for intelligent action and teaching appreciation. A skilled teacher knows that his or her comments and actions should model only fairness and inclusion and guide with appropriate outlets for humor. Educators who create an informal atmosphere where all are cherished and no place feels unsafe will change the culture of the school and the world no matter what race, orientation, disability, syndrome, income level, or status comes their way.

Gifted students are at an increased risk because it is easier to marginalize their pain. Educators have stereotyped them as being given more and getting more than other students, and the tactics used to bully them are thought of as funny or as not a big deal. Furthermore, gifted students often intellectualize their pain to the point that it becomes unbearable, exacerbating taunts into tragedy with no way to escape from the constant worry and fear. But with the use of small interventions, problem-solving strategies, and increased leadership roles given to these students, they can help others and advocate for themselves.

Educators must be well informed about bullying, as it is a topic they may need to discuss with parents given its prevalence. Educators and parents must be aware of signs of bullying and be ready to squelch it immediately should the need arise. Communication built on trust will pay dividends.

# TOOLS FOR DIGGING DEEPER

Dubin, N. (2007). *Asperger syndrome and bullying: Strategies and solutions.* London, UK: Jessica Kingsley.
Bullying is a serious problem of people with Asperger's syndrome, both at school and in the workplace, and displaying "different" behavior, such as not understanding social rules, exacerbates the risk of being victimized. This book describes bullying behavior and the danger of persistent recurrence if it remains unchecked, as well as the critical importance of involving the bystander. The author goes on to provide effective strategies to address bullies and bullying that can be applied by parents, professionals,

and schools, and individuals being bullied. He stresses the importance of peer intervention, empathetic teachers, and verbal self-defense.

Greene, R. (2009). *Lost at school: Why our kids with behavioral challenges are falling through the cracks and how we can help them* (2nd ed.). New York, NY: Scribner.
This is a groundbreaking approach for understanding and helping kids and transforming school discipline. Many schools treat frequent visits to the principal's office with detentions, suspensions, and expulsions, but these strategies are ineffective for most students. This book outlines a new course for a conceptual framework for behavioral changes—kids overcome their obstacles; the frustration of teachers, parents, and classmates diminishes; and the well-being and learning of all students are enhanced.

Tassell, B. (2006). *Don't feed the bully*. South Bend, IN: Llessat.
This is a fictional detective story aimed at ages 10–14. Hannibal Greatneck III, detective, sixth-grade student, and Handy to his friends, walks into William B. Travis Elementary and finds a cage in the middle of the classroom, with a sign on the cage reading "Don't feed the bully." A student is inside! The school has dealt with its bully problem by handing over all the power to another bully. Handy must find the clues, outwit the villains, and get control of William B. Travis back to the students and faculty. The story is a funny one with hilarious yet serious undertones but with great purpose.

Wiseman, R. (2002). *Queen bees & wannabes: Helping your daughter survive cliques, gossip, boyfriends and other realities of adolescence*. New York, NY: Three Rivers Press.
Who's in? Who's out? Who's cool? Who's not? Why is one girl elevated to royal status and another shunned? *Queen Bees & Wannabes* answers these unfathomable questions and so many more. Wiseman gives parents the insight, compassion, and skill needed to guide girls through the rocky terrain of the adolescent social world.

# CHAPTER 8

# Underachieving
# Gifted Students[2]

The phenomenon of underachievement is difficult to define and sometimes even more difficult to detect. Gifted underachievers are those who earn exceptional scores on standardized measures of achievement and aptitude but do not display this same level of achievement in school as evidenced by their grades or evaluations of their work (McCoach & Siegle, 2008). There are many possible reasons for this discrepancy between expected and actual achievement. Underachievement can be associated with social-emotional issues, a learning disability, physical interference, or a mismatch between curricula and ability. Despite the different causes of underachievement, underachievers exhibit similar behaviors that include "low academic self-perceptions or low self-efficacy, low self-motivation, low effort toward academic tasks, external attributions, low goal-valuation, and negative attitudes toward school and teachers" (McCoach & Siegle, 2008, p. 724). Clark (2008) identified the following characteristics of underachievers:

- Have a low self-concept; negative evaluations of self; feelings of inferiority demonstrated by distrust, indifference, lack of concern, and/or hostility toward others.
- Are socially more immature than achievers; lack self-discipline, procrastinate, refuse tasks deemed unpleasant; highly distractible; highly impulsive; unwilling to face realities and consequences.
- Have feelings of helplessness; may externalize conflict and problems, avoid challenges.

---

2    Rose Hatcher contributed to the development of this chapter.

- Do not see the relationship between their efforts and subsequent achievement outcomes; negate personal responsibility for failure.
- Are hostile toward adult authority figures; distrust adults in general.
- Have lower aspirations for future; lack future plans or career goals; resist goals that have been set for them.
- Perform at higher levels on tests that require synthesizing than on detailed, computational, or convergent problem-solving tasks that require precise and analytic information processing. (p. 371)

Teachers in classrooms and schools who focus on standardized high-stakes testing or do not offer curricula commensurate with a child's abilities and readiness can create "involuntary underachievers" (McCoach & Siegle, 2008, p. 727). These underachievers often have limited opportunities to engage in advanced curricula, complaining of boredom in school and becoming apathetic and disengaged from the learning process (Davis, 2010). Those schools most focused on high-stakes testing are those low-performing schools that often have minority student populations that are predominantly from low socioeconomic backgrounds (Bankston & Caldas, 2002). Teachers may also hold low expectations for students, be disingenuous, and lack empathy for student problems (Ford, 2011b).

Social-emotional issues impacting underachievement can include, but are not limited to, problems at home and issues with peers. Dysfunctional homes are often chaotic or unstable, which does not make for supportive learning environments and can cause distractions from learning and other behavioral issues. Such home environments are characterized by sibling rivalry, inconsistent expectations, and poor models of learning. Peer influence can be both positive and negative, especially over time, as although "being perceived as intelligent is often a social asset in elementary school, social pressure in middle and high school may influence gifted students to underachieve in order to camouflage their giftedness" (Hébert, 2011, p. 238). With intense pressure to fit in, particularly during adolescence, it is easy to understand why some students would succumb to the idea of being less smart.

Teachers play a significant role in reversing underachievement. Hébert (2011) suggested the following teacher behaviors made a difference in regards to academics:

- Took time to get to know the student before initiating an investigation [into the underlying causes of underachievement].
- Used their time with students to facilitate the process rather than counsel them regarding their underachievement.
- Saw their role as facilitator of the process. In doing so, they arranged conferences with the students, provided resources, allocated time for the students to complete the project, and offered suggestions when students seemed to be at a standstill.
- Understood that students needed to feel like participating professionals and share their products with authentic audiences.
- Recognized the dynamic nature of the underachievement program by observing students, reflecting on their behaviors as they worked on the projects, and identifying strategies to help them overcome problems.
- Consistently demonstrated patience and believed in the student. (p. 257)

# MEET JACKSON

Jackson is an identified gifted and talented second grader. His profile is presented here as a tool for identifying characteristics and strategies for addressing issues of underachievement that are both academic and behavioral in nature. If you were Jackson's teacher, where would you start and what would you do? What parental or family input would you seek? And how can both the teacher and parents work together to improve Jackson's situation?

The stapled five-sheet packet of paper is intact, except for the fact that it is torn into four thick curling strips with penciled scribbles and one large letter on the first page, looking more like a modern work of art than a writing assignment. This is the work (or more appropriately— nonwork) of Jackson. In his desk is an array of self-made cartoon books full of dialogue, ingenious characters, and detailed black-and-white illustrations. On a bulletin board display, there is an abstract drawing and a typed writing composition called "The Hungry Man" created by Jackson. The composition is cohesive, funny, detailed, and mechanically accurate. He can create his own PowerPoint presentations and has excellent auditory skills. On the other hand, he refuses to follow school rules or do assignments that he doesn't like, and he often hops around the classroom like a frog. Jackson is fortunate that he was identified as gifted at an early age, although the quality of his work has been totally erratic and unrepresentative of gifted students. What types of creative adaptations might a teacher make to help Jackson reveal his ability on a consistent basis and grow his potential?

Jackson is from a lower income family and lives at home with his mother, older sister, and younger brother. Jackson sees his father on weekends. There is some evidence of drug abuse in the family, and he shows signs of occasional hunger. Jackson was evaluated for gifted testing when he was in a regular second-grade classroom. His scores in the 99th percentile for both achievement and aptitude qualified him for gifted programming. Jackson's abilities are evident on standardized testing, yet his classroom work is most often incomplete or of poor quality.

A conversation between Jackson's teacher and his parent(s) would be important to help gain a greater understanding of Jackson's home life and background. If a face-to-face meeting cannot be arranged, a phone conversation also can help to complete a more holistic picture of Jackson's circumstances.

## ACKNOWLEDGING JACKSON'S UNDERACHIEVEMENT

Jackson's characteristics and behaviors are examples of underachievement. Like many gifted learners, Jackson qualified for gifted services in the second grade by exhibiting superior scores on measures of expected achievement. However, his subsequent performance in a self-contained gifted classroom demonstrated a severe discrepancy between expected achievement and actual achievement.

## ASSESSING JACKSON'S NEEDS BEYOND
## HIS ADVANCED ABILITIES

Jackson does very good work when it is something he wants to do. If he doesn't want to do the work, he becomes recalcitrant, stubbornly refusing to do his own work and interfering with his classmates' ability to work. In addition to his issues with schoolwork, he has wide mood swings in short periods of time, moving between manic excitement and sullen despair. Some of these behaviors seem to stem from the lack of a basic understanding of appropriate social skills. His home life seems to be chaotic and disjointed, and he sometimes expresses that he does not know where he is going to sleep or eat. Right in the middle of a deep concentration, he may decide to start talking or singing to himself, pull other students from their work, or just stop and start making one of his cartoon doodle books. Apart from behavior issues, there are deficits in his fine motor skills that are evident in Jackson's writing, and there is some indication that he struggles with fingering the strings of his violin. Although Jackson has very good reading skills—fluency, comprehension, and word recognition are excellent—his verbal skills are much weaker. He has a tendency to speak in a whisper-like voice, talk very fast, and use incomplete sentences. There also is a slight stutter.

These behavioral and learning issues suggest that he could profit from additional assessment for multiple exceptionalities. These assessments may reveal learning or social-emotional issues that require additional interventions. In order to arrange for these additional assessments, parental permission will be needed, and this would be a good opportunity to discuss with parents the reasons behind the assessment and what all parties can learn from the results.

Jackson's greatest and most volatile strength is his creativity. He definitely thinks out of the box and can quickly concretize ideas into projects and action. However, his lightning-quick creative constructs are often interrupted by his chaotic disturbances. Sometimes it's laughter and sometimes there is a "teachable moment" that exhilarates the whole class, and everyone twinkles with the excitement of spontaneous learning. More often than not, however, everyone is thrown off task and momentary hysterics emerge.

Recommendations for nurturing creative learners in the classroom include: establishment of a less restrictive school setting; active involvement; more challenging tasks; active inquiry; academics that are fun; avoidance of excessive competition with other children; engagement of fantasy; and the ability for students to pursue topics of strong interest (Kim, 2008).

The Response to Intervention Model (RtI) could also be an alternative intervention in order to identify Jackson's other possible learning needs. RtI is typically a three-tiered service-delivery model (National Research Center on Learning Disabilities [NRCLD], n.d.). When implemented successfully, RtI can assist in alleviating academic and behavioral issues. Tier 1 initiates "high-quality instruction and curriculum that will address the needs of approximately 80% of the students" (Pereles, Omdal, & Baldwin, 2009, p. 43). Based on this initial instruction, any of Jackson's identified educational needs are provided with prescribed interventions that are monitored (NRCLD, n.d.; Pereles et al., 2009). If the educational need persists (measured by curriculum-based measures [CBMs]), Tier 2 interventions are implemented: "the goal . . . is to provide supplemental instruction to students for whom Tier 1 instruction is insufficient" (NRCLD, n.d., para. 3). This multi-tiered system can respond with increasingly intensive interventions based on Jackson's needs, as determined through CBMs and observations by counselors and teachers. Tier 3 includes additional tailored instruction by a special education teacher and/or counselor, depending on the results of the ongoing needs assessment.

Pereles et al. (2009) found RtI to be more advantageous than traditional special education interventions, stating, "RtI . . . is more fluid than the typical school system of separate programs because all student needs, remedial and advanced, can be addressed" (p. 43).

By identifying Jackson's unmet educational and behavioral needs, perhaps his proclivity toward underachievement can be stemmed by introducing interventions in a more timely manner by concentrating on his strengths and addressing the areas of his learning profile that require remediation.

# CONCLUDING COMMENTS

Underachievement can be a difficult puzzle to unravel. Teachers and parents each can provide valuable information to each other about what happens at school and at home respectively. By gaining the most complete picture possible, appropriate interventions and strategies can be identified in order to meet a student's specific need to help reverse the underachievement. Reversing underachievement usually requires that parents and educators work together. The end result is worth the effort, as the child reverses both motivation and work ethic—important ingredients of a successful future.

# TOOLS FOR DIGGING DEEPER

"Giftedness and Academic Underachievement"
http://www.counselingthegifted.com/articles/underachieve.html
This article explains how targeted therapy helped a young man overcome his underachievement behaviors.

Gifted Underachievement: Root Causes and Reversal Strategies: A Practical Handbook for Guidance Counselors and Teachers
http://www.fultongifted.org/_doc/Gifted%20Underachievement%20Handbook.pdf
This document explains giftedness and underachievement while providing suggestions.

# CHAPTER 9

# Enhancing Collaboration Between Parents and Educators

I entered the classroom with the conviction that it was crucial for me and every other student to be an active participant, not a passive consumer . . . [a conception of] education as the practice of freedom . . . education that connects the will to know with the will to become. Learning is a place where paradise can be created.

—bell hooks

Barriers break down when information is available and correct—when myths about gifted children are debunked. Partnerships between parents and educators are built on trust and respect. Such collaboration is very important in order to give the children who are gifted and talented opportunities to soar. Learning is ongoing when children have no learning ceiling. They benefit when educators and parents collaborate and have excellence as a goal.

## MATCHING EXPECTATIONS

Collaboration is far more likely to occur when goals are shared and known to all parties. A principal described one strategy to encourage this sharing of goals. At the beginning of the school year, all parents and guardians were given a 3" x 5" card and were asked to write down what they most wanted their children to learn that year (Hoerr, 2012). The specific directions were: "What do you want for your child from our school? What's the one thing you want us to teach your child?" (Hoerr, 2012, p. 90). He discovered that communication increased when parents had the opportunity to write their goals for their children for the school year. He reported that it set a positive tone for the school and, consequently, enhanced learning.

Classroom teachers, special teachers (music, art, foreign language, and physical education teachers), librarians, resource teachers (both special education and gifted education), counselors, and principals benefit from such activities when they learn what parents hope for and expect for their children during that school year. Educators also benefit from learning as much as possible about the young people. They need to know a lot about the children in their classroom—what they spend their time doing when not in school, what they enjoy reading when a book is not assigned, and what type of assignments they enjoy most. The more the teachers and the curriculum leader in a school know about the children, the more the children are likely to learn each day they are in school. It is critically important that all teachers expect all children in their classrooms to be learning on an ongoing basis. Another way to express that view is that all children will be making continuous progress. In fact, a wonderful way for parents or guardians to communicate with teachers is to ask for evidence that the child is making continuous progress. Parent-teacher conferences are times to share information that documents learning since the last conference.

# EFFECTIVE COMMUNICATION STRATEGIES FOR COLLABORATION

Effective communication requires both parties to be good listeners and talkers. Effective communication is a two-way opportunity—absorbing information as well as providing information. It involves clarifying what the other person says in addition to asking questions. Good communication recognizes that parents and educators have an interest in seeing that the child does well in school and ends up being well prepared to be successful in life. They must work together, collaborating to allow the children to develop their potential and to become lifelong learners.

Two-way communication is most effective as teachers and parents conference. Lawrence-Lightfoot (2003) described effective communication in this passage:

> When teachers speak of telling the truths about their students through the vivid recall of an anecdote, through data gathering and documentation, and through the presentation of artifacts, they also know that a one-way presentation of information will never produce the trust that is the bedrock of productive parent-teacher encounters. Truth and trust grow out of a dynamic interaction in which listening for truths is just as important as telling them. (p. 9)

For all parties in the conversation, the central focus must be the child. The child's welfare is what brings parents and teachers together to conference.

A very important consideration in all schools is to create a welcoming environment for parents and other visitors. When school personnel make parents feel welcome, parents will be far more willing to come to school to learn about how to help their children thrive and prepare to be successful at the next level, whether it be middle or high school or postsecondary opportunities. Parents are far more likely to come talk with teachers than they would ever be otherwise. The first individuals with whom the parent may come in contact are often the secretary and others in the front office. That will be where the tone is set for the building. Teachers also can facilitate conversation with parents or limit the possibility of good communication by how they meet parents and words they choose.

Not all parents or adult family members have warm memories of their school experiences. Thus, an initial barrier may be trying to get the parent to come to school at all. Sometimes that is best accomplished through a school activity that is fun and welcoming. Such an experience can get the parent feeling comfortable being in the school.

For other parents it is the opposite problem—the parent volunteers to help in the classroom but no one calls to use the talents and time that the parent is willing to spend helping. There are so many ways that teachers can use volunteers, but it takes time on the teacher's part to organize to take advantage of the extra hands. It is well worth the teacher's time to do so. Parents can be used in numerous ways. They can work with students one-on-one or in a small group. They can be trained and lead Junior Great Book sessions. Parents can help a small group who are ready for enrichment activities that the teacher finds it difficult to find time to implement. They can prepare materials that take time to assemble, including setting up science experiments. This list can certainly be expanded to ensure that all children benefit from extra adults spending time in classrooms with the goal that all children make continuous progress. Of course, the long-term goal is for students to be successful in postsecondary educational opportunities and in what they do for their life's work.

In order to keep communication ongoing, words must be selected carefully. All parties remember well words that were cutting and/or spoken in anger or said thoughtlessly. The more specific one can be, the more likely the conversation is to lead to positive results. For example, parents do not want to hear only about the child's undesirable behaviors. Also, if a parent says that the child is bored, it is useful for the teacher to ask questions to get at the bottom of the statement. Asking what the child does when not in school can reveal interests that could be incorporated into assignments. Inquiring about the books the child reads at home can also be revealing of the level of reading that is motivating to the child. Such conversations can lead to possibilities for substituting assignments to make them a match for the child's level of readiness to learn.

# A PRINCIPAL'S PERSPECTIVE CONCERNING COMMUNICATION BETWEEN EDUCATORS AND PARENTS OF DIVERSE GIFTED LEARNERS

Dr. Mary Evans, principal of Cumberland Trace Elementary School in the Warren County Schools in Bowling Green, KY, provided the following tips for improving communication between educators and parents of gifted children from diverse backgrounds.

Parental involvement in children's schooling is a very important component in maximizing students' learning potential. Developing and maintaining good home/school communication is essential to building strong parent involvement. The concept of parent involvement has lots of support in research but is often difficult to put into practice, especially with diverse learners. The gap between research and reality is influenced by many factors such as parent and educator beliefs, the current life situations of families, parents' perceptions of their "place" in schools based on past experiences, and the differing agendas of parents and educators. The barriers to the development of effective parent involvement must be addressed, and opening avenues of communication is the way to begin.

The first barrier to overcome for successful home/school communication relates to attitudes of school staff, misunderstandings, and lack of information. Professional development on topics such as working with students and families from disadvantaged homes, twice-exceptional learners, and meeting the needs of students who are learning the English language is essential in helping school staff understand the obstacles that must be overcome in order for these students to learn at appropriately high levels. Educators who have knowledge about the differences among learners can then work together to find ways to address diverse needs. Familiarity with linguistic and cultural backgrounds as well as with economic and attitudinal issues helps educators understand why parents are not able to support their children in the traditional ways such as helping with homework, signing paperwork, and attending parent/teacher conferences.

Overburdened educators working in schools with large class sizes, dwindling resources, and increased student performance demands may not feel they have the time or expertise to communicate with parents who do not respond to notes or e-mails because of time, literacy, or language constraints. This is where support staff with interest in diverse learners and their families can step in to bridge the communication gaps. Family Resource Center (a service provided for families of lower income children in Kentucky schools) personnel are invaluable for connecting with families through home visits, arranging transportation to school meetings, and providing for basic needs such as food and clothing. They can be the liaisons between the family and the school as they mentor parents in understanding schools and provide important feedback to the school about the needs of the family.

Parents of disadvantaged children often do not recognize that their children have exceptional potential because learning gaps due to frequent moves prevent their children from bringing home report cards with high grades. It takes one significant adult to recognize the untapped learning potential in a child and find a way to fill in the learning gaps. An adult can offer encouragement by talking with the child and provide opportunities for challenge. This happened for a quiet, reserved fifth-grade student named Esra who attended our school for one year. Esra's teacher nominated her for the Academic Team, a quick-recall team that competes in various content areas, and she qualified to participate. Esra's father was a truck driver who was seldom home during the week, and Esra's mother did not have a car. School personnel took on the responsibility of taking Esra home after practices and scrimmage meets. Esra was a vital member of the Academic Team and received lots of recognition among her peers and her self-concept improved. She began to participate more in class, gained a wide circle of friends, and showed great academic success.

Increased accountability with universal screenings and progress monitoring ensure that schools have pages and pages of diagnostic and summative information about students' abilities and achievement. This information is often shared at parent/teacher conferences or sent home in folders in backpacks.

Parents with transportation issues, work conflicts, or language barriers do not have the benefit of sitting down with a teacher and having their child's scores explained. A teacher, counselor, or administrator must take the time to communicate this important information to families.

One summer day after school was out, as I was reviewing standardized achievement data, I noticed extremely high scores for a fourth grader, LeAnn, who had poor school attendance. I knew LeAnn and had tutored her after school because she frequently did not have her homework done. I decided to give the family a call and congratulate them on LeAnn's high scores. The father was clearly touched by the phone call and thanked me for making him aware that his daughter was highly capable. A few days later the father called and asked me to explain to him again what the scores indicated and asked what he should do to help his daughter earn more high scores. These conversations began a home/school partnership that resulted in finding donors to provide a scholarship for LeAnn to participate in a Super Saturday program at a local university and in finding a community mentor through the Big Brother Big Sister Program.

Standardized test scores and teachers educated about the characteristics of twice-exceptional children will result in finding students who have disabilities in some areas and advanced abilities in other areas. Finding these students can make a huge positive difference in the self-concept of these students and in their academic success. For example, Liza's exceptional math ability was shown on a standardized achievement test. Her former teachers knew she was stronger in mathematics than in reading but did not recognize her as being gifted in that area because she struggled so much with word problems. When Liza's principal congratulated her on being selected for a gifted program in the area of mathematics, Lisa exclaimed, "I knew I was smart! I knew I was smart! How did you find out?" Liza's secret was out, and she thrived with the opportunities that she was provided to develop her math ability.

Sometimes parents recognize these dual exceptionalities and bring them to the attention of the school. It is very important that the parents and teachers have a strong working relationship and keep the lines of communication open to meet the diverse needs of these students. They will need to collaborate to develop educational plans that nurture the child's strengths and provide support in the area of disability. This may require great flexibility of scheduling so that the students can participate in both special education and gifted pull-out programs, and it may require modifications in the gifted services by providing support in the area of the disability so that the student can soar in his or her area of strength.

The challenge of identifying gifted children and providing them with appropriate educational services is particularly complex when they are English language learners. The process of second language acquisition is long and complex, and it is difficult to determine a child's intellectual potential by using English-based assessment instruments. Teachers who work most closely with these students, such as English as a Second Language (ESL) teachers, are usually the first to notice high potential, which is often shown in the speed and skill with which students learn a new non-English-based game. Three Burmese elementary students who spent their early years in a refugee camp in Thailand quickly became very adept at the game of chess. An instructional assistant for the ESL classroom offered to provide transportation home for the Burmese students so they could join the Chess Team.

ESL teachers can serve as advocates for their students as they meet with regular classroom teachers. They often know when children serve as "interpreters" for the family and miss school to accompany parents to meetings or doctors' appointments. Sometimes elementary English learners cannot stay after school for enrichment activities because they are needed to take care of younger siblings at home while parents work. Parents of English language learners may distrust any "special" classes—including classes for the gifted and talented—because they know of English language learners who are misplaced in special education classes due to language issues. Families are more willing for their children to participate in gifted programs when the gifted program is seen as an opportunity for students to work harder and learn more. When a parent or relative is an illegal immigrant, the child may fear authority figures and not want to build relationships with teachers and other helpful adults in the school. All of these barriers have to be accepted and communication with parents approached with care and sensitivity.

The most common ways of sharing information with parents (e.g., packets of reading materials, parent newsletters, parent awareness meetings) take advanced planning in order to provide the information translated in the native language. Schools can join with outreach workers from local International Centers, universities, and churches to communicate with families. Subscribing to media services that provide interpreters in a variety of languages can be well worth the cost.

Schools must establish a welcoming climate that encourages understanding, sensitivity, and appreciation of diversity. Society and schools benefit when the learning goals of diverse learners are identified and talent potential is nurtured. Facilitating effective communication between the school and the parents is essential in order for educators and parents to work as a team to provide appropriate educational opportunities for all children, including diverse learners.

# PROFESSIONAL DEVELOPMENT NEEDED FOR PARENTS AND EDUCATORS

Parents need to know where to find information that will help them learn what is true and what is myth about gifted children as well as about strategies for helping their children in school. A school can create a section in the library that has parent materials available for checkout. Educators or parents can also hold parent sessions during school or after school. Sometimes it is helpful to have such sessions during school hours so school-age children will be engaged without need for childcare for those children. There may still be a need to have childcare for younger children during the sessions.

Planning for and offering professional development at the school or district levels would be an important step in building understanding and support for twice-exceptional children and English language learners as well as other children who have been historically underrepresented in programming for gifted children. The professional development does not have to occur in a one-day or a half-day workshop, although that could be the way to get started. The professional development might be 10-minute information sessions at faculty meetings. It might include putting a short article in mailboxes (actual mailboxes or e-mail inboxes) and then scheduling time to discuss the article at the next faculty meeting. It might include having a Professional Learning Community lead the way with a focus on twice-exceptional learners, children from lower income families, or students who are culturally diverse. Learning about diverse gifted children might also occur at a professional conference or by visiting a school with outstanding programming in one or several of these areas. The key point, of course, is that educators must all increase their awareness of these children's existence and needs and add to their repertoire of skills and knowledge to let these young people learn on an ongoing basis and feel positive about themselves as individuals in the classroom and school communities.

## CONCLUDING COMMENTS

Collaboration between educators and parents works best when they share goals for the children and the climate of the school and classroom is welcoming for the parents. Communication is most effective when conversation is two way and ongoing—not a one-time event. One strategy that is important to remember is to concentrate on the positive or the strengths while also shoring up or supporting areas of weakness—but the strengths must remain the first priority in working with students.

# TOOLS FOR DIGGING DEEPER

Rimm, S. (2007). *Keys to parenting the gifted child* (3rd ed.). Scottsdale, AZ: Great Potential Press.
This book describes useful strategies to share with parents, many of which are also appropriate for educators.

Robinson, A., Shore, B. M., & Enersen, D. L. (2007). *Best practices in gifted education: An evidence-based guide*. Waco, TX: Prufrock Press.
This resource provides information about best practices in the home as well as in the classroom and the school.

# CHAPTER 10

# A Call to Action

The United States is squandering one of its most precious resources—the gifts, talents, and high interests of many of its students. In a broad range of intellectual and artistic endeavors, these youngsters are not challenged to do their best work. This problem is especially severe among economically disadvantaged and minority students, who have access to fewer advanced educational opportunities and whose talents often go unnoticed.

—*National Excellence: A Case for Developing America's Talent*

Each chapter in this book has provided information about children who are advanced, gifted, or talented yet diverse and often underrepresented in programming for children with gifts and talents. They are not represented or are underrepresented for various reasons, but a prominent reason is a lack of accurate information that would lead educators to recognize talent or advanced abilities in children who are culturally diverse, from lower income families, from families in which English is not the first language, or who are twice-exceptional learners. These children may also be from rural or urban areas, or perhaps in classrooms with teachers who do not recognize that they have gifted children. Advanced abilities do not have a chance to reveal themselves unless the learning experiences and expectations give children opportunities to demonstrate their advanced thinking abilities.

# REPORTS HIGHLIGHTING THE NEED TO PREPARE DIVERSE LEARNERS FOR BRIGHT FUTURES

Preparing young people who are both gifted and diverse for a successful future is in the best interest of the young people, as well as society at large. Various national reports address the need to develop our country's talent to the highest levels and implement policies that will guide our school districts, states, and country in doing so.

*Preparing the Next Generation of STEM Innovators: Identifying and Developing Our Nation's Human Capital* (National Science Board, 2010) made three recommendations:

- Provide opportunities for excellence. We cannot assume that our Nation's most talented students will succeed on their own. Instead, we must offer coordinated, proactive, sustained formal and informal interventions to develop their abilities. Students should learn at a pace, depth, and breadth commensurate with their talents and interests and in a fashion that elicits engagement, intellectual curiosity, and creative problem solving— essential skills for future innovation.

- Cast a wide net to identify *all* types of talents and to nurture potential in *all* demographics of students. To this end, we must develop and implement appropriate talent assessments at multiple grade levels and prepare educators to recognize potential, particularly among those individuals who have not been given adequate opportunities to transform their potential into academic achievement.

- Foster a supportive ecosystem that nurtures and celebrates excellence and innovative thinking. Parents/guardians, education professionals, peers, and students themselves must work together to create a culture that expects excellence, encourages creativity, and rewards the successes of all students regardless of their race/ ethnicity, gender, socioeconomic status, or geographical locale. (pp. 2–3)

Each of these recommendations of the National Science Board has several policy actions that accompany it. One of the recommended policy actions is to "create a national campaign aimed at increasing the appreciation of academic excellence and transforming stereotypes toward potential STEM innovators" (National Science Board, 2010, p. 31). This report is focused on STEM talent development; however, recommendations to provide opportunities for excellence, to cast a wide net in identifying all types of talent and to nurture potential in all demographics, and to foster a supportive environment for the development of talent are equally applicable for talent development in all talent areas. The recommendations can be instrumental in communicating the importance of talent development to parents, educators, and leaders in professional organizations and business and industry, as well as decision-makers in schools districts, state houses and state legislative bodies, and at the national level in the executive branch and Congress.

*Preparing the Next Generation of STEM Innovators* (National Science Board, 2010) highlighted the importance of developing talent as a way to ensure equality of opportunity. Equity and excellence are goals that are mutually supportive.

> Efforts to raise the educational achievement for all students must not only be continued in earnest, but accelerated. However, to reach *true* equality of opportunity, and to ensure that potential does not go unrealized, we must not overlook the educational needs of our Nation's most talented and motivated students. Too often, U.S. students with tremendous potential to become our future innovators go unrecognized and undeveloped. The dual goals of raising the floor of base-level performance and elevating the ceiling for achievement are not mutually exclusive. The Board believes that both equity *and* excellence are not only possible and mutually reinforcing, but necessary to achieve the American ideal. (National Science Board, 2010, p. 10)

*Mind the (Other) Gap!: The Growing Excellence Gap in K–12 Education* (Plucker et al., 2010) noted that there has been progress in reducing the achievement gaps in general, but there has been a lack of progress in reducing the excellence gap. The report is "intended to provide some preliminary excellence gap data and kick start the national discussion on the importance of excellence in our national and state K–12 education systems" (Plucker et al., 2010, p. 1).

> The goal of guaranteeing that all children will have the opportunity to reach their academic potential is called into question if educational policies only assist some students while others are left behind. Furthermore, the comparatively small percentage of students scoring at the highest level on achievement tests suggests that children with advanced academic potential are being under-served, with potentially serious consequences for the long-term economic competitiveness of the U.S. (Plucker et al., 2010, p. 1)

This report stated, "NAEP [National Assessment of Educational Progress] results suggest that the excellence achievement gaps among different racial groups, high- and low-socio-economic status, different levels of English language proficiency, and gender groups have widened in the era of NCLB" (Plucker et al., 2010, p. 4). One of the recommendations from *Mind the (Other) Gap!* is to "make closing the excellence gap both a national and state priority" (Plucker et al., 2010, p. 30). The excellence gap has not yet been the topic of discussion among many decision-makers. Unless decision-makers know about the excellence gap, they will not address this critical gap, and many of the problems described in this book will continue. The first step in closing the excellence gap is to make decision-makers aware that an excellence gap exists. Educators and parents can "kick start" that discussion and launch an awareness campaign.

One recommendation from *Mind the (Other) Gap!* that can be implemented and that would raise the awareness of the need to set excellence as an education goal is to ask these two basic questions whenever policies and other educational decisions are being discussed at the school, district, state, or national levels: "How will this affect our brightest students? How will this help other students begin to achieve at high levels?" (Plucker et al., 2010, p. 30).

Educators (classroom and special teachers, principals, counselors) can enhance the possibility that the excellence gap will be addressed when they get into the habit of thinking about these questions whenever decisions are being considered. The challenge at various levels of educational decision making is that the emphasis has been focused on minimum competencies for so long that keeping the focus on proficiency has become a habit. That focus will not reduce the excellence gap, as basic proficiency is an inappropriate goal for children who are advanced, gifted, and/or talented. Proficiency is grade-level learning. Of course, proficiency is a most appropriate goal for children who have not yet attained that level of achievement. However, proficiency becomes a holding pattern for learners when it remains the end-goal for all children in the class, even those who have demonstrated that they know and can do what is expected at the level of proficiency.

# CALL FOR ACTION: EXCELLENCE AND TALENT DEVELOPMENT

In order to prepare for a bright future, it is imperative to set talent development and excellence as priorities in schools across the United States. Recognizing talent in all areas is essential if talents are to be developed. Talents need to be recognized and developed in science, mathematics, writing, language arts, computer science, history, political science, art, music, drama, and dance. Individuals with outstanding potential in various content and talent areas include all socioeconomic backgrounds and all cultures as well as children who are twice-exceptional. Educators who make talent development their priority will set excellence as the goal and never be satisfied with proficiency or grade-level achievement for children who are ready to learn more. A focus on talent development will remove the lid from learning.

The following recommended actions are necessary to reach the goals of excellence and talent development:

- Messages about establishing talent development and excellence as educational goals must be clear and supported by policies at school district, state, and national levels.

- Professional organizations must partner with business and industry to garner support and to deliver the message that talent development is a priority. Excellence in a wide variety of domains must be the goal.
- Professional development must be offered to educate parents and educators about advanced, gifted, and talented children and young people—their diversity as well as their needs and strategies to foster interests and develop talents.
- All children, including those who are gifted, talented, and advanced, must have ongoing opportunities to learn at appropriately challenging levels and to pursue learning experiences to develop promise.

The Association for the Gifted (2009) stated:

We must believe that by dealing with the issues surrounding diversity and excellence in education, our country will be stronger. By committing to develop the great variety of gifts and talents of our nation's youth, we enhance both their potential and the potential of our country. (p. 8)

Parents and educators must collaborate about talent development and excellence. Often this collaboration starts with conversations. However, it cannot stop at that level if talent development and excellence are to become priorities in schools, school districts, states, and the nation. Parents and educators must also collaborate to establish an advocacy agenda to reduce and eliminate the excellence gaps. They must ensure that talent development is a reality for all children who are advanced, gifted, and/or talented. There is an immediate need to embrace the goals of talent development and excellence in education for children and youth from diverse backgrounds and to shift thinking to establish talent development and excellence as priorities.

# Resources[3]

## SUMMER AND SATURDAY SCHOOLS AND DISTANCE LEARNING

**G&T Programs**
http://www.nsgt.org/resources/programs.asp
Links to a variety of online, summer, and enrichment programming are provided at the National Society for the Gifted and Talented's website, including national and international resources. Links to different universities will lead parents and educators to other resources such as distance learning schools and family programs.

**Summer and Saturday Enrichment Programs**
http://www.hoagiesgifted.org/summer.htm
Hoagies' Gifted Education Page offers a list of enrichment programs taking place during the summer or on Saturdays at various institutions in the U.S. and worldwide. Programs are conveniently listed by location with information about age and grade levels. Links will take parents and educators directly to program sites for scheduling and enrollment information.

---

3    This section was contributed by Desiree R. Cho.

# COMPETITIONS

**Art Contests for Kids**
http://www.art-made-easy.com/art-contests-for-kids.html
Art . . . Made Easy! provides information about visual arts competitions
for kids. Parents and educators can sign up for a free e-mail newsletter
that has up-to-date information on contests. Those caring for and teaching talented art students will be interested in the lessons and resources
included on the site.

**FIRST**
http://www.usfirst.org
FIRST, which stands for "For Inspiration and Recognition of Science
and Technology," hosts various robotics and tech challenges for students
as young as 6 years old. Potential participants can easily search for a team
in their region on an interactive map.

**Headliners Performing Arts Competition & Championship**
http://www.headlinerscompetition.com
This is the only competition that enables dancers to qualify to represent
the U.S. at the World Show Dance and World Hip Hop Championships.
Age divisions range from 9 to 16+, and there are a variety of categories ranging from ballet and pointe to hip-hop and contemporary dance
styles. There is even a category for young choreographers.

**HP CodeWars**
http://www.hpcodewars.org
Hewlett-Packard hosts an annual computer programming competition
in Houston, TX, for high school students. Its site includes information
on the event, as well as sample problems that previous competitors have
encountered. There is also a link that allows schools to register their
students.

**MATHCOUNTS**
https://mathcounts.org
Information on competing in MATHCOUNTS's competitions can be

found on this website. Additional features include a problem of the week, a school handbook, information on past competitions, and videos for coaches and students.

## MENTOR: National Mentoring Partnership

http://mentoring.org

Serving students ages 6–18, MENTOR: The National Mentoring Partnership provides program resources for mentors and mentees on its website. Those interested in mentoring programs will especially appreciate the resources provided on safety and criminal background checks.

## MTNA Competitions

http://www.mtna.org/programs/competitions

The Music Teachers National Association provides information on performance and composition competitions for students. Information about competing can be found by first clicking on "Programs," and then selecting "Competitions." Doing so will bring visitors to a drop-down menu of states. Upon selection, the site will retrieve a list of competition dates and locations.

## National Academic Quiz Tournaments

http://www.naqt.com/index.html

NAQT is an organization that organizes national quiz bowls at the middle school, high school, community college, and university levels. Its website includes information about competing at the various levels as well as a series of articles under the "You Gotta Know . . ." tab that can help teams prepare.

## National Ocean Sciences Bowl

http://www.nosb.org

The Consortium for Ocean Leadership sponsors the National Ocean Sciences Bowl (NOSB) competition for high school students to test various aspects of the marine sciences, including biology, chemistry, physics, and geology. An interactive map under the "Competitions" drop-down menu leads potential participants to information for their states.

## NFL Competition Events

http://www.nflonline.org/AboutNFL/Events

In addition to accessing information about the National Forensic League's main debate events, viewers can download an official guide to competition events. Useful links about competing can be found on the left-hand side of the screen.

## Odyssey of the Mind

http://odysseyofthemind.com

Odyssey of the Mind is internationally known for promoting creative problem solving. Participants include students in kindergarten all the way through college. Click on "Regional Tournaments" for information on local chapters. Other helpful links include practice problems and classroom activities.

## Olympiads

http://www.k12academics.com/academic-competitions/olympiads

K12 Academics shares information about the official International Biology, Chemistry, Mathematical, and Physics Olympiad competitions in addition to the U.S. Biology and National Chemistry Olympiads. Users can access brief histories about the competitions and learn about how to participate.

## Scholarship & Competitions

http://www.arts-nsal.org/scholarships-and-competitions.shtml

The National Society of Arts and Letters is a nonprofit organization whose goal is to create opportunities for young artists. Competitions in musical theatre, drama, art, and literature are just some of these opportunities. Other links the site bring visitors to information on scholarships, master classes, and membership.

## Scripps National Spelling Bee

http://www.spellingbee.com

The E.W. Scripps Company is a media company that supports the longest-running spelling bee in the U.S. Links for teachers, students, and parents and information about enrolling in the competition are included on the website.

**USA Computing Olympiad**
http://www.uwp.edu/sws/usaco
The University of Wisconsin-Parkside hosts the USA Computing Olympiad to promote precollege computing. Useful links include information for teachers and first-time competitors about registration and training.

**Young Scientist Challenge**
http://www.youngscientistchallenge.com
Discovery Education and 3M sponsor this challenge for students in grades 5–8. Students compete individually, rather than in teams, creating videos about their problem-solving designs. Finalists have the opportunity to attend 3M's Summer Mastership Program to develop an invention under the guidance of a 3M scientist. Past winners have been awarded the opportunity to speak before members of Congress, the chance to work with directly with scientists to pursue a career in the sciences, and various monetary prizes.

# PERIODICALS AND NEWSLETTERS

*Parenting for High Potential*
http://www.nagc.org/index.aspx?id=1180
According to the National Association for Gifted Children, the organization that publishes this magazine eight times a year, *Parenting for High Potential* (*PHP*) is "for parents who want to make a difference in their children's lives." Packed with advice about developing a child's gifts and talents to the fullest, each issue includes special features, expert advice columns, and ideas from parents of high-potential youngsters.

*Teaching for High Potential*
http://www.nagc.org/index.aspx?id=1498
The National Association for Gifted Children publishes *Teaching for Higher Potential* (*THP*). Teachers will appreciate the practical tips and

materials focused on high-ability learners included in every issue. Each article is linked to supporting resources on the NAGC website.

# BOOKS

Assouline, S. G., & Lupkowski-Shoplik, A. (2005). *Developing math talent: A comprehensive guide to math education for gifted students in elementary and middle school* (2nd ed.). Waco, TX: Prufrock Press.

Assouline and Lupkowski-Shoplik discuss myths society may have about students who are mathematically gifted and offer suggestions aimed at parents and advocacy. Chapters on identification, assessment, programming, curricula, and teaching are included for teachers and administrators. An entire chapter is also dedicated to case studies that showcase information in previous chapters.

Berger, S. L. (2006). *College planning for gifted students: Choosing and getting into the right college.* Waco, TX: Prufrock Press.

Students, parents, and teachers alike will appreciate this resource. The book emphasizes the importance of matching the student to the right program while learning about colleges and going through the application process. Useful appendices include information on early entrance programs, SAT and ACT resources, and checklists for planning a student's junior year in high school.

Corwin, M. (2001). *And still we rise: The trials and triumphs of twelve gifted inner-city students.* New York, NY: HarperCollins.

Corwin is a reporter for the *Los Angeles Times* who spent a year with the students featured in his book. The urban setting in which these tenacious students live is the backdrop for their troubles and triumphs. Their stories will be inspiring to parents and teachers of gifted students as well as students in the same situation.

Daniels, S., & Piechowski, M. M. (Eds.). (2008). *Living with intensity: Understanding the sensitivity, excitability, and the emotional develop-*

*ment of gifted children, adolescents, and adults.* Scottsdale, AZ: Great
Potential Press.
Daniels and Piechowski focus on the emotional needs of gifted individuals over their lifespan, outlining Dabrowski's theory of development and
excitability and sharing practical applications for helping gifted individuals with excitability cope with sensitivities. Short and long forms for
assessing overexcitability are included.

Davis, J. L. (2010). *Bright, talented, and black: A guide for families of
    African American gifted learners.* Scottsdale, AZ: Great Potential
    Press.
Davis discusses how families can help Black students understand their
giftedness in the context of also being African American. Navigation of
peer relationships, underachievement, and the school system are discussions families and educators alike will find useful.

Fonseca, C. (2011). *101 success secrets for gifted kids: The ultimate guide.*
    Waco, TX: Prufrock Press.
This book's target audience is children ages 8–12 who want to know
more about being gifted. An explanation of what it means to be gifted
and the ensuing implications for school, friends, and home are included.

Fonseca, C. (2011). *Emotional intensity in gifted students: Helping kids
    cope with explosive feelings.* Waco, TX: Prufrock Press.
Fonseca discusses "what it really means to be gifted" and examines the
implications of giftedness for parents and teachers. The book includes
case studies and role-plays as well as worksheets and tip sheets to help
children manage various aspects of their giftedness such as stress manage-
ment, underachievement, perfectionism, and social anxiety.

Galbraith, J. (2000). *You know your child is gifted when . . .: A beginner's
    guide to life on the bright side.* Minneapolis, MN: Free Spirit.
Galbraith's book is for anyone—not just parents—who wants to know
more about gifted children. Parents showcase the traits, difficulties, and
joys of giftedness with various anecdotes, employing a good sense of
humor and jargon-free language.

Galbraith, J. (2009). *The gifted kids' survival guide: For ages 10 & under* (3rd ed.). Minneapolis, MN: Free Spirit.
Galbraith's book is written for younger gifted students who may be wondering about their giftedness. It explains what being gifted means and offers information on navigating gifted programs, social relationships, and interpersonal issues.

Jolly, J. L., Treffinger, D. J., Inman, T. F., & Smutny, J. F. (Eds.). (2011). *Parenting gifted children: The authoritative guide from the National Association for Gifted Children.* Waco, TX: Prufrock Press.
This book is an excellent resource for anyone wanting to know more about how to identify a gifted child, how gifted children develop, the diversity of gifted children, and programming options for teaching a gifted child.

Kerr, B. A., & Cohn, S. J. (2001). *Smart boys: Talent, manhood, & the search for meaning.* Scottsdale, AZ: Great Potential Press.
Parents and educators of gifted males will be interested in a number of issues covered in this book: development from youth to adulthood, underachievement, social aspects of being a gifted male, and suggestions for guiding them academically and emotionally.

Kiesa, K. (Ed.). (2000). *Uniquely gifted: Identifying and meeting the needs of the twice-exceptional student.* Gilsum, NH: Avocus.
This book discusses the needs of twice-exceptional students. A variety of perspectives are explored, as family members, parents, teachers, researchers, and administrators have contributed. Educators and families of twice-exceptional students will discover they are not alone despite their unique situations.

Murkoff, H., Eisenberg, A., & Hathaway, S. (2009). *What to expect the first year* (2nd ed.). New York, NY: Workman.
This series includes books on gestation but also has works on child development. This particular book includes information particular to parents and families of newborns: breastfeeding, selecting a physician, and home

safety. Early childhood care providers and parents will be interested in the material on monthly developmental milestones, illness, and first aid.

Murkoff, H., & Mazel, S. (2011). *What to expect the second year: From 12 to 24 months.* New York, NY: Workman.
This is an excellent resource about caring for toddlers. Topics of interest include information on caring for children when they become ill, home safety, and developmental disorders. Those caring for precocious children will be particularly interested in chapters on behavior, talking, and learning.

Neihart, M., & Poon, K. (2009). *Gifted children with autism spectrum disorders.* Waco, TX: Prufrock Press.
This book includes useful information for parents and educators about the characteristics and needs of this unique population of gifted learners. Educational strategies, intervention, and placement are discussed.

Neihart, M., Reis, S. M., Robinson, N. M., & Moon, S. M. (Eds.). (2001). *Social and emotional development of gifted children: What do we know?* Waco, TX: Prufrock Press.
The editors have included chapters discussing a wide variety of topics in gifted education, such as acceleration, social and emotional issues, perfectionism, and underachievement. Practices, interventions, and recommendations for gifted children's social and emotional development are noted.

Rimm, S. (2003). *See Jane win for girls: A smart girl's guide to success.* Minneapolis, MN: Free Spirit.
In her previous books written for adults, *See Jane Win* and *How Jane Won*, Rimm surveyed more than 1,000 successful women. This book, however, was written for gifted girls and includes stories from kids and teens. Tips for building healthy self-esteem, finding mentors, and learning are given. Quizzes and questions will engage young readers.

Schultz, R. A., & Delisle, J. R. (2006). *Smart talk: What kids say about growing up gifted.* Minneapolis, MN: Free Spirit.

This book provides an excellent look at giftedness from the perspective of children ages 4–12. Presented in an easy-to-read question-and-answer format, *Smart Talk* covers issues such as what it means to be gifted, social situations with friends, expectations of others, school, family, individual interests, and future plans.

Siegle, D., (2005). *Developing mentorship programs for gifted students.* Waco, TX: Prufrock Press.

This book is an excellent resource for those wanting to start a mentoring program for students. Chapters include information on why mentoring is important, how to develop a program, and how to select mentors and mentees. Monitoring a program once it is underway is also discussed.

Smutny, J. F., Walker, S. Y., & Meckstroth, E. A. (1997). *Teaching young gifted children in the regular classroom: Identifying, nurturing, and challenging ages 4–9.* Minneapolis, MN: Free Spirit.

This is a great resource for teachers of young students. Identification of the young gifted child, creation of a welcoming learning environment, and compaction and extension of the curriculum are discussed. Additional topics are broken down by subject area. Assessment, groupings, communication between parents and teachers, students' social and emotional needs, and diverse populations are also addressed.

Sousa, D. A. (2009). *How the gifted brain learns.* Thousand Oaks, CA: Corwin Press.

In addition to explaining what being gifted means, Sousa's book is an excellent resource that discusses how to challenge gifted students. He discusses differentiation, the use of acceleration and curriculum compacting, and instructional processes such as Bloom's taxonomy and independent studies. Information on underachievement, twice-exceptional students, and domain-specific giftedness is also noted.

VanTassel-Baska, J. L. (Ed.). (2010). *Patterns and profiles of promising learners from poverty.* Waco, TX: Prufrock Press.

VanTassel-Baska introduces readers to the various patterns and profiles associated with promising learners from poverty. Other contributors look at the role that culture, geography, and ethnicity play on a gifted child. Recommendations for educators working with urban, rural, and low-income students are discussed.

Walker, S. Y. (2002). *The survival guide for parents of gifted kids: How to understand, live with, and stick up for your gifted child.* Minneapolis, MN: Free Spirit.

Walker's book is meant for parents and those who desire to better understand a parent's point of view. She discuss myths such as "It's a snap to raise a gifted child" and "Gifted kids will make it on their own," as well as the programming available and how to advocate for a gifted child.

Webb, J. T., Amend, E. R., Webb, N. E., Goerss, J., Beljan, P., & Olenchak, F. R. (2005). *Misdiagnosis and dual diagnoses of gifted children and adults: ADHD, bipolar, OCD, Asperger's, depression, and other disorders.* Scottsdale, AZ: Great Potential Press.

This is an excellent resource that looks at giftedness in occurrence with a variety of other issues: ADD/ADHD; anger diagnoses; ideational and anxiety disorders; mood disorders; learning disabilities; sleep disorders, allergies, asthma, and reactive hypoglycemia; and relationship issues. An entire chapter is dedicated to differentiating gifted behaviors from pathological behaviors, and another includes information on seeking health-care professionals and/or counselors.

Webb, J. T., & Gore, J. L. (Eds.). (2004). *Grandparents' guide to gifted children.* Scottsdale, AZ: Great Potential Press.

Webb and Gore frame the traits and needs of the gifted child in the context of a grandparent's relationship with his or her grandchild. Topics are pertinent to general audiences in the section "Areas of Concern for Gifted Children" but also include information specific to grandparents in "Avoid Being a Pushy Grandparent."

Willis, J. A. (2009). *Inspiring middle school minds: Gifted, creative, & challenging.* Scottsdale, AZ: Great Potential Press.

Willis is a classroom teacher and M.D. who specializes in neurology. Thus, her book provides a unique perspective on educating the middle-school-aged child. In addition to looking at neurology during adolescence, she discusses middle school classrooms and ways to extend and enrich learning.

# WEBSITES

**AEGUS**

http://www.aegus1.org

The Association for the Education of Gifted Underachieving Students is an advocacy group serving underachieving gifted students. Its website includes information abut its annual conference and resources for those who want to know more about the special needs of gifted children.

**CEC**

http://www.cec.sped.org

The Council for Exceptional Children prides itself on being "the leading voice for special and gifted children." Although there is a membership fee to join CEC, its website includes access to information on news and issues, policy and advocacy, and professional development.

**Cool Math**

http://www.coolmath.com

This website includes information on a variety of math topics from pre-algebra to calculus. Educators and parents will be interested in the math lessons, and students will enjoy the games that encompass skills ranging from basic computation to spatial reasoning and logic. Best of all, the site covers other topics including reading and spelling, geography, and science.

**Davidson Institute for Talent Development**

http://www.davidsongifted.org

The Davidson Institute was formed in 1999 to serve profoundly gifted young people. Its programs and services include scholarships, a summer institute, and resources for parents and educators. Information on the Davidson Academy, a free public school for profoundly gifted students, is also included.

### Discovery Channel

http://dsc.discovery.com

The Discovery Channel's website includes information on its shows, but educators and parents will want to scroll to the bottom of the home page to find related sites: Discovery Kids, Discovery Education, Student Competitions, and Discovery Channel Videos. Students of all ages can take advantage of information on a variety of science and social studies-related topics.

### History Channel

http://www.history.com

The History Channel includes videos teachers may find useful for the classroom as well as a link to events for "This Day in History." Students will enjoy games that include a timeline puzzle, quizzes, and interactive encyclopedias such as "Dinopedia." Topics are broken down by categories such as science and technology, U.S. Presidents, women's history, and various wars and eras.

### Hoagies' Gifted Education Page

http://www.hoagiesgifted.org

Hoagies' Gifted Education Page has resources for parents, educators, and kids. Parents will appreciate information on characteristics of gifted children and schooling options, and educators can find information on professional development and special topics in gifted education. Students will enjoy links to reading lists, movie reviews, and recommended software and toys.

### On-Line Math Worksheet Generator

http://themathworksheetsite.com

Families and teachers in need of extending and/or enriching a student's math skills will find The Math Worksheet Site useful for basic computation skills, fractions, measurement, graphing on coordinate planes, and telling time. The site also has an option to create a "one hundred chart" starting at either 0 or 1. For an extra fee, individuals and schools can subscribe to the site, gaining access to worksheets for other skills such as place value, fact families, geometry, simple statistics, radicals and exponents, logarithms, and geometry.

**Museums in the USA**

http://museumca.org/usa

This website claims to house the most developed online museum information network of any country in the world and includes a variety of ways to search for museums: by name, state, and location. The database links readers to the museums' websites and recommends places to visit.

**National Association for Gifted Children**

http://www.nagc.org

An excellent resource for parents and educators, NAGC's site lists information on gifted education by state. Additional information of interest includes upcoming conventions and seminars as well as legislation related to gifted students.

**National Geographic Kids**

http://kids.nationalgeographic.com/kids

This website includes an easy-to-navigate home page with drop-down menus for topics such as games, videos, animals and pets, photos, and countries. Parents and teachers of younger students will appreciate the "Little Kids" menu, which includes science experiments and crafts for primary learners.

**PBS Kids**

http://pbskids.org

The Public Broadcasting System page for kids includes thinking games that are appealing to younger children. Parents will appreciate the link to PBS Parents, which has information on child development and children's health, as well as advice on lighter topics such as birthday parties. Educators will find useful information by grade level on the PBS Teachers page. All pages include a link back to the PBS home page, which has television programming schedules and information organized by topic.

**Science for Kids**

http://www.acs.org

Parents and educators will find want to click on the "Education" drop-down menu at the American Chemical Society's (ACS) home page to access resources, student programs, and information on bachelor's degrees endorsed by ACS. Students will enjoy the "Science for Kids" link under the "Education" tab, which provides access to experiments, information on the periodic table, activities, games, and puzzles for elementary through high school ages.

### Starfall
http://www.starfall.com
Starfall Education's website has games both for children who are ready to read and for young students who are already reading. Students can play games to learn letter sounds as well as read stories and create avatars to tell about themselves. Poetry, tongue twisters, and riddles are included, and parents and educators may benefit from practice pages and journals, which can be downloaded for free.

### SENG
http://www.SENGifted.org
The website for the organization Supporting Emotional Needs of the Gifted includes links to articles and other resources of interest to parents and educators of gifted children. A box to subscribe to SENG's free e-mail newsletter is at the middle of the home page, and drop-down tabs about programs, parent groups, and continuing education can also be found.

### Telementor
http://www.telementor.org
The International Telementor Program facilitates mentorships for students in grades K–12 and beyond. Communication between mentors and mentees is project-centered. Families and educators can use the site to find mentors and learn about available projects.

### The Association for the Gifted (CEC-TAG)
http://www.cectag.org
This website provides valuable information about children with gifts and talents. It highlights information about those children from diverse back-

grounds who traditionally may be underrepresented in gifted programming, including children who are twice-exceptional.

**Zoos in the USA**
http://www.officialusa.com/stateguides/zoos
For students interested in wildlife and conservation, this site enables parents and educators to search for zoos by state. Other links include access
to sites such as the American Zoo and Aquarium Association and the
American Sanctuary Association.

# References

Adams, C. M., & Olszewski-Kubilius, P. (2007). Distance learning and gifted students. In J. L. VanTassel-Baska (Ed.), *Serving gifted learners beyond the traditional classroom* (pp. 169–188). Waco, TX: Prufrock Press.

Assouline, S. G. (Summer, 2010). Understanding twice-exceptionality. *Talent,* 1–3.

Baldwin, A. Y. (2004). Introduction to culturally diverse and underserved populations of gifted students. In A. Y. Baldwin & S. M. Reis (Eds.), *Culturally diverse and underserved populations of gifted students* (pp. xxiii–xxxi). Thousand Oaks, CA: Corwin Press.

Bankston, C. L., & Caldas, S. J. (2002). *A troubled dream: The promise and failure of school desegregation in Louisiana.* Nashville, TN: Vanderbilt University Press.

Clark, B. (2008). *Growing up gifted: Developing the potential of children at home and at school* (7th ed.). Upper Saddle River, NJ: Pearson.

Colangelo, N., Assouline, S. G., & Gross, M. U. M. (2004). *A nation deceived: How schools hold back America's brightest students* (Vol. 1). Iowa City: The University of Iowa, The Connie Belin & Jacqueline N. Blank International Center for Gifted Education and Talent Development.

Davidson Institute for Talent Development. (2006). *Tips for parents: Finding a mentor for your gifted child.* Retrieved from http://www.davidsongifted.org/db/Articles_id_10283.aspx

Davis, J. L. (2010). *Bright, talented, & Black.* Scottsdale, AZ: Great Potential Press.

Dubin, N. (2007). *Asperger syndrome and bullying: Strategies and solutions.* London, UK: Jessica Kingsley.

Fisher, A. Q., & Rivas, M. E. (2001). *Finding fish*. New York, NY: William Morrow.

Ford, D. Y. (2011a). *Multicultural gifted education* (2nd ed.). Waco, TX: Prufrock Press.

Ford, D. Y. (2011b). *Reversing underachievement among gifted Black students* (2nd ed.). Waco, TX: Prufrock Press.

Grantham, T., & Ford. D. Y. (2003). Providing access for culturally diverse gifted students: From deficit thinking to dynamic thinking. *Theory Into Practice, 42*, 217–225.

Hébert, T. P. (2011). *Understanding the social and emotional lives of gifted students*. Waco, TX: Prufrock Press.

Hickam, H. H. (1998). *Rocket boys*. New York, NY: Delacorte Press.

Higher Education Opportunity Act, P.L. 110-315 (2008).

Hodgkinson, H. (2000). *Secondary schools in a new millennium: Demographic certainties, social realities*. Reston, VA: National Association of Secondary School Principals.

Hoerr, T. R. (2012). What are parents thinking? *Educational Leadership, 69*, 90–91.

Individuals with Disabilities Education Improvement Act, Pub. Law 108-446 (December 3, 2004).

Johnsen, S. K. (Ed.). (2011a). *Identifying gifted students: A practical guide* (2nd ed.). Waco, TX: Prufrock Press.

Johnsen, S. K. (2011b). Introduction to the NAGC pre-K–grade 12 gifted programming standards. In S. K. Johnsen (Ed.), *NAGC pre-K–grade 12 gifted education programming standards: A guide to planning and implementing high-quality services* (pp. 1–26). Waco, TX: Prufrock Press.

Johnsen, S. K., Feuerbacher, S., & Witte, M. M. (2007). Increasing the retention of gifted students from low-income backgrounds in university programs for the gifted: The UYP Project. In J. L. VanTassel-Baska (Ed.), *Serving gifted learners beyond the traditional classroom* (pp. 55–80). Waco, TX: Prufrock Press.

Kim, K. H. (2008). Underachievement and creativity: Are gifted underachievers highly creative? *Creativity Research Journal, 20*, 234–242.

Kingsolver, B. (2002, Winter). Congratulatory letter. *The Challenge, 8,*

9. Retrieved from http://www.wku.edu/DepartSupportAcadAffairs/
Gifted/ giftedsite/wordpress/wp-content/uploads/2010/07/811.pdf

Lawrence-Lightfoot, S. (2003). *The essential conversation*. New York, NY:
Random House.

Loveless, T., Farkas, S., & Duffett, A. (2008). *High-achieving students in
the era of No Child Left Behind*. Washington, DC: Fordham Institute.

McCoach, D. B., & Siegle, D. (2008). Underachievers. In J. A. Plucker
& C. M. Callahan (Eds.), *Critical issues and practices in gifted education* (pp. 721–734). Waco, TX: Prufrock Press.

MENTOR. (n.d.). *Elements and toolkits*. Retrieved from http://www.
mentoring.org/program_resources/elements_and_toolkits

Myers, W. D. (2001). *Bad boy: A memoir*. New York, NY: Harper Collins.

National Association for Gifted Children. (2010a). *NAGC pre-K–grade
12 gifted programming standards: A blueprint for quality gifted education programs*. Washington, DC: Author.

National Association for Gifted Children. (2010b). *Redefining giftedness
for a new century: Shifting the paradigm*. Retrieved from http://www.
nagc.org/index.aspx?id=6404&terms=Redefining+Giftedness

National Education Association. (2006). *The twice-exceptional dilemma*.
Washington, DC: Author.

National Research Center on Learning Disabilities. (n.d.). *What is RTI?*
Retrieved from http://www.nrcld.org/topics/rti.html

National Science Board. (2010). *Preparing the next generation of STEM
innovators: Identifying and developing our nation's human capital*.
Arlington, VA: National Science Foundation.

No Child Left Behind Act, P.L. 107-110 (Title IX, Part A, Definition
22) (2002).

OECD. (2011). *Against the odds: Disadvantaged students who succeed in school*. Retrieved from http://www.pisa.oecd.org/
dataoecd/6/12/47092225.pdf

Olszewski-Kubilius, P. (2007). The role of summer programs in developing the talents of gifted students. In J. L. VanTassel-Baska (Ed.),
*Serving gifted learners beyond the traditional classroom: A guide to alter-
native programs and services* (pp. 13–32). Waco, TX: Prufrock Press.

Olweus, D. (1993). *Bullying at school: What we know and what we can do*.
Cambridge, MA: Blackwell.

Pereles, D. A., Omdal, S. N., & Baldwin, L. (2009). Response to Intervention and twice-exceptional students: A promising fit. *Gifted Child Today, 32*(3), 40–51.

Plucker, J. A., Burroughs, N., & Song, R. (2010). *Mind the (other) gap! The growing excellence gap in K–12 education.* Retrieved from http://ceep.indiana.edu/mindthegap

Riley, T. L., & Karnes, F. A. (2007). Competitions for gifted and talented students: Issues of excellence and equity. In J. L. VanTassel-Baska (Ed.), *Serving gifted learners beyond the traditional classroom* (pp. 145–168). Waco, TX: Prufrock Press.

Roberts, J. L. (2008). Multiple ways to define academic success: What resonates with you? *The Challenge, 21,* 12–13.

Rosen, P. (Producer & Director). (2010). *A surprise in Texas: The thirteenth Van Cliburn international piano competition* [documentary]. United States: Van Cliburn.

Ryser, G. R. (2011). Fairness in testing and nonbiased assessment. In S. K. Johnsen (Ed.), *Identifying gifted students: A practical guide* (2nd ed., pp. 63–74). Waco, TX: Prufrock Press.

Sklare, G. (2005). *Brief counseling that works: A solution-focused approach for school counselors and administrators* (2nd ed.). Thousand Oaks, CA: Corwin Press.

Southern, W. T., & Jones, E. D. (2004). Types of acceleration: Dimensions and issues. In N. Colangelo, S. G. Assouline, & M. U. M. Gross (Eds.), *A nation deceived: How schools hold back America's brightest students* (Vol. 2, pp. 5–12). Iowa City: The University of Iowa, The Connie Belin & Jacqueline N. Blank International Center for Gifted Education and Talent Development.

The Association for the Gifted, Council for Exceptional Children. (2009). *Diversity and developing gifts and talents: A call to action.* Retrieved from http://www.cectag.org

Toppo, G., & Elias, M. (2009). *Lessons from Columbine: More security, outreach in schools.* Retrieved from http://www.usatoday.com/news/education/2009-04-13-dolumgin3-l3wwonw_N.htm

Trump, K. (2011). *Creating an anti-bullying program with resources you have.* Retrieved from http://www.districtadministration.com/article/create-anti-bullying-program-resources-you-have

U.S. Department of Education, Office of Educational Research. (1993). *National excellence: A case for developing America's talent.* Washington, DC: U.S. Government Printing Office.

Weinfeld, R., Barnes-Robinson, L., Jeweler, S., & Shevitz, B. R. (2006). *Smart kids with learning disabilities: Overcoming obstacles and realizing potential.* Waco, TX: Prufrock Press.

Wyner, J. S., Bridgeland, J. M., & DiIulio, J. J. (2007). *Achievement trap: How America is failing millions of high-achieving students from lower-income families.* Lansdowne, VA: Jack Kent Cooke Foundation.

# About the Authors

**Julia Link Roberts**, Ed.D., is the Mahurin Professor of Gifted Studies at Western Kentucky University. She is the Executive Director of The Center for Gifted Studies and the Carol Martin Gatton Academy of Mathematics and Science in Kentucky. Dr. Roberts is a member of the Executive Committee (Treasurer) of the World Council for Gifted and Talented Children and a board member of the Kentucky Association for Gifted Education and The Association for the Gifted (a division of the Council for Exceptional Children). Dr. Roberts was honored with the 2011 Acorn Award, given to an outstanding professor at a Kentucky college or university. She received the first David W. Belin NAGC Award for Advocacy. She is coauthor, with Tracy Inman, of *Strategies for Differentiating Instruction: Best Practices for the Classroom* (winner of the 2009 Legacy Award for the outstanding book for educators in gifted education by the Texas Association for the Gifted and Talented) and *Assessing Differentiated Student Products: A Protocol for Development and Evaluation*. Dr. Roberts and her daughter Julia Roberts Boggess coauthored *Teacher's Survival Guide: Gifted Education* and *Differentiating Instruction With Centers: Gifted Education*. Dr. Roberts directs summer and Saturday programs for children and young people who are gifted and talented and teaches graduate courses in gifted education. Dr. Roberts and her husband, Richard, live in Bowling Green, KY. They have two daughters, Stacy and Julia, and four granddaughters, Elizabeth, Caroline, Jane Ann, and Claire.

**Jennifer L. Jolly**, Ph.D., received her doctorate in educational psychology with a concentration in gifted education from Baylor University. Currently she is an assistant professor in elementary and gifted education at Louisiana State University. Her research interests include the history of gifted education and parents of gifted children. She also serves as editor-in-chief of NAGC's *Parenting for High Potential*. Before her tenure at LSU, she taught in both gifted and regular education classrooms as a public school teacher.

# About the Contributors

**Desiree R. Cho** graduated from Concordia College in Moorehead, MN, with a bachelor's degree in elementary education and a major in English literature. She has been fortunate to teach across grade levels in regular, special, and gifted education settings. Currently, she is pursuing her doctorate at Louisiana State University.

**Rose Hatcher** is a graduate of Louisiana State University, Baton Rouge. She became a public school teacher at the age of 55 after a successful career in real estate and facilitating creativity workshops in California, Louisiana, and Canada. Mrs. Hatcher currently teaches third-grade gifted students in a self-contained classroom. She is especially interested in encouraging the expression of raw creativity in children.

**Brad Tassell** is the best-selling, award-winning author of *Don't Feed the Bully*, which is read by thousands of students in school every year. He is the recipient of three 2011 Pinnacle Awards for his anti-bullying programs for students and teachers. He can be contacted at http://www.bullyspeaker.org.

**Janet Hagemeyer Tassell, Ph.D.,** is an assistant professor in the School of Teacher Education at Western Kentucky University and was the recipient of the college's Teaching Award and Research/Creativity Award. Specializing in mathematics education and gifted education, Dr. Tassell has taken her experience as a mathematics teacher and as Director of Learning and Assessment for a rural school district and brought her unique skills to WKU. She and her husband, Brad, are the proud parents of their wonderful daughter, Darby.

# The Association
# for the Gifted

For more than 50 years, The Association for the Gifted (TAG), as a Division of the Council for Exceptional Children (CEC), has been the leading voice for special and gifted education and is devoted to twice-exceptional children, educational excellence, and diversity. CEC-TAG establishes professional standards for teacher preparation for the field, develops initiatives to improve gifted education practice, and ensures that the needs of children and youth with exceptionalities are met in educational legislation. To learn more about TAG and to become an active member, visit http://www.cectag.org.